THE FIRSTBORN

THE
FIRSTBORN

A Play in Three Acts

BY

CHRISTOPHER FRY

CAMBRIDGE

At the University Press

1946

CAMBRIDGE
UNIVERSITY PRESS

University Printing House, Cambridge CB2 8BS, United Kingdom

Published in the United States of America by Cambridge University Press, New York

Cambridge University Press is part of the University of Cambridge.

It furthers the University's mission by disseminating knowledge in the pursuit of education, learning and research at the highest international levels of excellence.

www.cambridge.org
Information on this title: www.cambridge.org/9781107629226

First published 1946
First paperback edition 2014

A catalogue record for this publication is available from the British Library

ISBN 978-1-107-62922-6 Paperback

To

MY MOTHER
and
MY BROTHER

CONTENTS

CHARACTERS

ANATH BITHIAH, *Pharaoh's sister*

TEUSRET, *Pharaoh's daughter*

SETI THE SECOND, *the Pharaoh*

RAMASES, *his son*

MOSES

AARON, *his brother*

MIRIAM, *his sister*

SHENDI, *Miriam's son*

Two overseers, a Minister (KEF)
A guard and a servant

The action of the play takes place in the summer of 1200 B.C.,
alternating between Pharaoh's palace and Miriam's tent

THE FIRSTBORN

✤

ACT ONE
SCENE ONE

The terrace of the palace of Seti the Second, at Tanis. A morning in the summer of 1200 B.C. *A flight of steps (unseen) leads down through a gate to open ground. The terrace looks out upon an incompleted pyramid.*

A scream.

Enter from the palace ANATH BITHIAH, *a woman of fifty, sister to the Pharaoh, and* TEUSRET, *a girl of fifteen, the Pharaoh's daughter*

Anath. What was it, Teusret?

Teusret.   Did you hear it too?

Anath. Some man is dead. That scream was password to a grave.
Look there: up go the birds!

Teusret.   The heat on this terrace!
You could bake on these stones, Aunt Anath.

Anath.   Ask who it was.

Teusret. They're working steadily at father's tomb.
There's no sign of trouble.

Anath.   We're too far off to see.
We should know more if we could see their faces.

Teusret (calling down the steps). Guard! Come up here.

Anath.   I should like to be certain.
Oh, that pyramid! Everyday, watching it build,
Will make an old woman of me early.
It will cast a pretty shadow when it's done.
Two hundred more men were taken on to-day,

Did you know that, Teusret? Your father's in a hurry.
Their sweat would be invaluable to the farmers in this drought.
What pains they take to house a family of dust.

Teusret. It's a lovely tomb.

Anath.   Yes, so it may be.
But what shall we do with all that air to breathe
And no more breath? I could as happily lie
And wait for eternal life in something smaller.

(*Enter* A GUARD)

Teusret. What was that scream we heard?

Guard.   It's nothing, madam.

Anath. You are right. Nothing. It was something once
But now it is only a scare of birds in the air
And a pair of women with their nerves uncovered;
Nothing.

Teusret. Who was it screamed?

Guard.   One of the builders
Missed his footing, madam; merely an Israelite.
They're digging him into the sand. No, over to the left.

Teusret. Oh yes, I see them now.—That was all I wanted.

(*Exit* THE GUARD)

So that's all right.

Anath.   Can you remember your cousin?

Teusret. Why, which cousin?

Anath.   My foster son. You knew him
When you were little. He lived with us in the palace.

Teusret. The birds are back on the roof now.

Anath.   Moses, Teusret.

Teusret. What, Aunt? Yes, I think I remember. I remember
A tall uncle. Was he only a cousin?
He used to drum his helmet with a dagger
While he sang us regimental marches to get us to sleep.
It never did. Why?

Anath.   No reason. I thought of him.
Well, they've buried the man in the sand. We'd better
Find our morning again and use what's left.
  Teusret. Why did you think of him? Why *then* particularly?
  Anath. Why not then? Sometimes he blows about my brain
Like litter at the end of a public holiday.
I have obstinate affections. Ask your father.
He would tell you, if it wasn't impolitic
To mention Moses, what a girl of fire
I was, before I made these embers.
He could tell you how I crossed your grandfather,
And your grandfather was a dynasty in himself.
Oh Teusret, what a day of legend that was!
I held forbidden Israel in my arms
And growled on my stubborn doorstep, till I had my way.
  Teusret. What do you mean?
  Anath.   Well, never mind.
  Teusret.   I do.
You've told me so far.
  Anath.   Keep it to yourself then.
The summer of '24 had brilliant days
And unprecedented storms. The striped linen
You once cut up for a doll's dress was the dress
Made for me that summer. It was the summer
When my father, your grandfather, published the pronouncement.
  Teusret. What pronouncement?
  Anath.   That all the boys of Jewdom
Should be killed. Not out of spite, Teusret; necessity.
Your grandfather ordered that Defence of the Realm be painted
At the head of the document, in azure and silver.
It made it easier for him.
  Teusret.   Were they killed?
  Anath. Yes, they all died of a signature. Or we thought so,

Until the thirtieth of August. I went bathing on that day.
I was a girl then, Teusret, and played with the Nile
As though with a sister. And afterwards as I waded
To land again, pushing the river with my knees,
The wash rocked a little ark out
Into the daylight: and in the ark I found
A tiny weeping Israel who had failed
To be exterminated. When I stooped
With my hair dripping on to his face
He stopped in a screwed-up wail and looked.
And when I found my hands and crowded him
Into my breast, he buried like a burr.
And when I spoke I laughed, and when I laughed
I cried, he was so enchanting. I was ready
To raise a hornet's nest to keep him; in fact
I raised one. All the court flew up and buzzed.
But what could they do? Not even my Pharaoh-father
Could sting him out of my arms. So he grew up
Into your tall cousin, Egyptian
From beard to boots and, what was almost better,
A soldier of genius. You don't remember
How I held you on this terrace, to see him come home from war?
It was ten years ago. Do you remember
The shrieking music, and half Egypt shouting
Conqueror! Peacemaker!

 Teusret.   No.

 Anath.   They have all tried to forget.
They have blotted him out of the records, but not out
Of my memory.

 Teusret. Why did they blot him out?
I can never get at the truth of what came next.
I sometimes overhear his name muttered
In the corridors, between servants or the soldiers.

But when they see me they stop their conversation.
I have seen my father fidget at the name of a battle
And change the subject. What is it all about?
Moses was a prince of this house, my cousin.
Now he is someone not to be spoken of.
"The murder" I've heard them say, and "Since the murder".
What did he do? Did he go mad or something?

   Anath. I might have known that I should say too much.

   Teusret. Aunt, you must tell me.

   Anath.   Well, no doubt I meant to.
The day I held you here, he came as the conqueror
Of Abyssinia. In all the windows and doors
Women elbowed and cracked their voices; and men
Hung on the gates and the trees; and children sang
The usual songs, conducted by their teachers.
As for me, nothing would stop me shaking.
As for him, as for Moses, he was as tired
As a dog, and stumbled when he climbed the steps to the palace.
There was a brilliant reception. He was decorated
By your grandfather.

   Teusret.   Yes, but what happened to make him—

   Anath. All right, I'm coming to it, Teusret. The day after,
For the country-side also to be able to see the hero,
He went to inspect the city being built at Pithom.—
My book was closed from that day forward.
He went round with an officer who unfortunately
Was zealous but unintelligent. Silly man:
Silly, silly man. He found a labourer
Idling or resting, and he thought, I suppose,
"I'll show this prince that I'm worth my position"
And beat the workman. A Jewish bricklayer.
He beat him senseless.

   Teusret.   And then?

Anath.   What happened then
I only know out of the sleepless nights
Which I endured afterwards. In those nights
I made myself a knowledge, and believe it.
Moses turned—turned to what was going on—
Turned himself and his world turtle. It was
As though an inward knife scraped his eyes clean.
The General of Egypt, the Lion and the Prince
Recognized his mother's face in the battered body
Of a bricklayer; saw it was not the face above
His nursery, not my face after all.
He knew his seed. And where my voice had hung till then
Now voices descending from ancestral Abraham
Congregated on him. And he killed
His Egyptian self in the self of that Egyptian
And buried that self in the sand.

Teusret.   Aunt—
                    (*Enter* a guard)
Guard.   The Pharaoh.
Madam, the Pharaoh is here.
Anath.   Can we look innocent?
            (*Enter* seti. *Exit* the guard)
Teusret. Good morning, father.
Seti.   Go indoors, my Teusret.
                                    (*Exit* teusret)

Anath. Is the day such vexation? Did you listen to me
And sleep apart from your empire for one night?
You didn't. Egypt has argued in the dark again
While the night struck bitter bells on every clock.
Look at you! Your eyes are deaf with listening
To your wretched pillows, Seti.
Seti.   Where is Moses?
Anath. Seti!

Seti.   Where is Moses? You will know.
In what country? Doing what?
 Anath.   Why Moses?
 Seti. I need him.
 Anath.   I've no reason to remember.
I'm without him.
 Seti.   But you know.
 Anath.   Why should I know?
Why should I? When the sun goes down do I have to know
Where and how it grovels under the world?
I thought he was a dust-storm we had shut outside.
Even now I sometimes bite on the grit.
 Seti. Time has made it easier. The men are dead
Who wanted his death-sentence. I must have him home.
 Anath. Indeed you've not slept!
 Seti.   I have found him necessary.
Libya is armed along the length of her frontier,
And the South's like sand, shifting and uncertain.
I need Moses.—We have discarded in him
A general of excellent perception.
 Anath. He's discarded, rightly or wrongly. We've let him go.
 Seti. Deeds lie down at last, and so did his.
Out in the wilderness, after two days' flight,
His deed lay down, knowing what it had lost him.
Under the boredom of thorn-trees his deed cried out
For Egypt and died. Ten years long he has lugged
This dead thing after him. His loyalty needn't be questioned.
 Anath. We're coming to something strange when a normal day
Opens and lets in the past. He may remember
Egypt. He's in Midian.
 Seti.   In what part of Midian?
 Anath. Wherever buckets are fetched up out of wells
Or in his grave.

Seti. We'll find him. If we have to comb
Midian to its shadows we'll find him.

Anath. He's better where he is.

Seti. He is essential to my plans.

Anath. I tell you
He is better where he is. For you or me
He's better where he is.
We have seen different days without him
And I have done my hair a different way.
Leave him alone to bite his lips.

Seti. He and I
Were boys who went well together, in spite of a difference
In age. He was old for his years. We were excellent friends.

Anath. Boys go home from school. After a time
All boys become initials cut in wood.

Seti. Prepare yourself to see him back.

(*His eye is caught by something below and beyond the terrace*)

What's this,
What is this crowd?

Anath. It's Ramases! No qualms
For the dynasty, with a son as popular as he is.

Seti. There's half the city round him. Where are his guards?

Anath. There: a little behind.

Seti. The boy's too careless
Of himself. This mobbing is a fever and out of proportion.
You would think he had brought them a conquest; he might be a hero
The way they cheer him. They're even climbing the gates
To see him come through. What is the matter with you?

Anath. What do you mean?

Seti. You're shaking.

Anath. Nonsense, Seti.

Seti. I'm not altogether at rest in the way he's growing,

Not altogether pleased with his free-and-easy good humour,
His good graces for no-matter-whom.
The young have keys that we have lost. They enter
Life by doors which were better never unlocked.
This easily-come-by popularity, for instance,
Is a danger above all dangerous to princes.
I don't like his drift or trust his politics.

Anath. What are his politics?

Seti.   Exactly so;
What are they? There are no politics more dangerous
Than politics that don't seem to exist.
I can trust my enemy, trust him to be my enemy,
But Ramases follows unpredictable instincts.
They'll turn on him one of these days, like lion-cubs
Who play so innocently and later on
Find a mouth for blood. He must learn to abdicate
His heart and let the needs of Egypt rule there.

Anath. He will learn. He is learning.

Seti.   Egypt should pray so.

Anath. I would hazard a guess that Egypt's women
Have prayed for him often enough. Ra, raising
An eyebrow stiff with the concentration of creation
Probably says: That boy again? We'd better
Make something of him early and have them satisfied.
O, Ramases will be all right.

Seti.   I hope,
I hope.

                    (*Enter* RAMASES, *a boy of eighteen*)

Ramases. Did you see the excitement? I think it's the drought.
Like the air, we're all quivering with heat.
Do you find that, Aunt? Either you must sleep like the dead
Or something violent must happen.

Anath.   Look: your father.

Ramases. I didn't see you, father. I'm sorry, sir.
Did I interrupt state matters?

   Seti.   If they had been,
We should have fetched you here. What morning have you had?

   Ramases. Holiday—books rolled up, military exercises
Over, and no social engagements. I've been fowling
Down at the marshes.

   Anath.   Any luck?

   Ramases.   Not much flesh
But a paradise of feathers. I was out before daybreak.

   Anath. It's a good marksman who hunts by batlight.

   Ramases.   But I
Waited for daylight. Until then the marsh was a torpor.
I clucked and clapped as the sun rose
And up shot so much whistle and whirr
I could only hold my spear and laugh.
All the indignant wings of the marshes
Flocking to the banner of Tuesday
To avoid the Prince of Egypt!
Off they flapped into the mist
Looking about for Monday
The day they had lived in peace: and finding nothing
Back they wheeled to Tuesday.
I had recovered myself by then and killed
One that had the breast of a chestnut.
At last he could feel the uninterrupted darkness
Of an addled egg. I watched his nerves flinching
As they felt how dark that darkness was.
I found myself trying to peer into his death.
It seemed a long way down. The morning and it
Were oddly separate,
Though the bird lay in the sun: separate somehow
Even from contemplation.

Anath.   Excellent spirits
To make a success of a holiday.
  Ramases.   Only for a moment.
  Seti. This afternoon I have business for you. (*He turns to go in*)
  Ramases.   Very well.
  Seti. Was that thunder?
  Anath.   They're dumping new stone for the pyramid.
  Ramases. Two men came through the marshes before I left;
Jews, but not our Jews: or one of them
Was not; he seemed a man of prosperity
Although some miles of sun and dust were on him.
  Seti. Aliens?
  Ramases.   Yes; but one of them I felt
I should have known. I stared but couldn't place him.
He stood so strongly up out of some recollection
And yet what was it? How could I have known him?
I passed them again as I came home. They stood
To watch the crowd. I looked across and smiled
But got no smiles from them. They looked, and yet
They seemed to look back in their minds
Rather than out at me. And one, the tall one—
  Anath. Very tall?
  Ramases.   Yes, he was tall. It was he
Who is somehow in my memory.
  Anath.   Seti—
  Seti.   Well?
  Anath. Is it possible that someone hasn't waited to be recalled?
Is it possible?
  Seti.   It is not possible.
  Anath. Your thoughts are leaning that way too.
Sometimes the unaccountable stalks in.
  Seti. Which way were they travelling, Ramases?
  Ramases. This way. If I had only thought of them sooner

We could have seen them go by.—Sir!
They are standing here at the foot of the stairway. How long
Can they have been there? They're standing without moving,
Gazing up: not conversing, but looking up:
Who let them through? Shall I speak to them?

Anath. He has stood all day under my brain's stairway.
Seti, who is there? Which foremost, Ramases?
The tall one?

Ramases.   Yes. Who's in your mind?

Anath.   The tall one.
The tall one.

(RAMASES *goes down the steps*)

           So he is back; and small-talk
Has to block a draught up ten years old.
God help me.

Seti.   Why has he come?

Anath.   You said he longed
For Egypt.

Seti.   I think so.

Anath.   But what am I in Egypt?
A dead king's daughter.

(*Re-enter* RAMASES, *followed by* MOSES *and* AARON)

Seti. I am tempted to call this a visitation and not
A visit. What words can I find to fit
So ghostly a homecoming?

Ramases (*to* ANATH).   Who is this man?

Seti. Understand you are welcome. Whatever uncertainty
You have can go. We welcome you. Look who is here.

Anath. He has seen me. We have looked at one another.

Seti. We'll absolve ourselves of the ten years. Who is this?

Moses. My brother.

Seti.   I had not heard you had a brother.

Anath. A brother, a sister—and a mother. All the three.

Seti. Our lives at their most coincidental bring the gods
Very near. I told my sister we must have you back.
And so we must, and so Egypt must; and it seems
That we have. You are come promptly at the word, Moses.

   Moses. This is not why I came.

   Seti.   You would scarcely foresee it.

   Moses. I am not who you think. I am a stranger.

   Seti. Not by a vein or a hair. The past is forgotten.
You are a prince of Egypt.

   Moses.   The prince of Egypt
Died the day he fled.

   Seti.   What do you mean?

   Moses. That prince of Egypt died. I am the Hebrew
Smitten out of the shadow of that prince,
Vomited out of his dry lips, the cry
Whipped off the sanded tongue of that prince of Egypt.

   Seti. What has this long discomfort done for you,
My friend? It has made you bitter.

   Moses.   Make no mistake;
I have done very well for myself. I haven't come to beg.
Why was it you decided to ask me to come back?

   Seti. Isn't it time we laid the crippling ghost
That haunts us? You evidently thought so too
To come so far.

   Moses.   You've a better reason than that.

   Seti. Why should you want reasons when you have come
On your own initiative? Why are you here?
I am asking you candidly. Why did you come?

   Moses. My blood heard my blood weeping
Far off like the swimming of fear under the sea,
The sobbing at night below the garden. I heard
My blood weeping. It is here it wept and weeps.
It was from here I heard coming this drum of despair,

The hidden bullfrog of my brothers' grief:
Under your shoes, under your smile, and under
The foundations of your tomb. From Egypt.

  Anath. What was it, Seti, that lay down and died?

  Seti. Why are you here?

  Moses.   To be close to this
That up to now has only made me uneasy,
As though a threat of evil whispered beyond
Control under the wind. I could be
Uneasy and still eat in Midian.
I could be Pharaoh in Midian, but in Egypt
I knew I should be Moses.

  Seti.   Still you haven't
Answered my question. Come, what do you want?

  Moses. First, that you should know what you are doing.

  Seti. Take care, Moses.

  Anath.   And secondly?

  Moses.   What can I hope
From that until he has understood the first?

  Seti. What is this mood you have come in which is so ready
To abuse a decent welcome? There is something shipwreck
About you that will not do for peaceful places.
Steady yourself if we're to understand one another.
I am the Pharaoh, Moses, not the young uncle
Of the Heliopolis classroom, nor your messroom brother.
Well, go on.

  Moses.   A man has more to be
Than a Pharaoh. He must dare to outgrow the security
Of partial blindness. I'm not speaking now
To your crown; I'm speaking to your merciless mischief.

  Seti. You have coarsened during your exile. What you say
Hasn't even the virtue of clarity. If you wish
To consider my offer of reinstatement, go

And consider. I can be patient. Egypt can do
Her work on you like a generous woman, given
Her time. (*He glances at Anath*)
        Midian will wash off in the Nile.
Go on, go on, I shall not remember this morning.

  Moses. I think you will. My brother has lived these days
In amongst Israel, while I was sleeping.
He knows both the truth and the injury better than I can.
He has had refuge, this last year, close to your border.
He was hunted out for his friendship to flesh and blood,
And so he has lain with his ear against the door
Hearing pain but unable to come to it.
He stands here with me now so that what shall be said
Shall be truthfully said and what you shall hear
Will have earned hearing because the teller lived it.

  Aaron. Twelve hundred thousand Israelites are under
Your dominion. Of these two hundred and twenty thousand
Only, are men. The rest are in the proportion
Of four hundred and fifty thousand women
And five hundred and thirty thousand children.

  Seti. I have my census-takers.

  Aaron.   So perhaps
Has Death got his; but I think he has not referred
His undertakings to your dynastic understanding.
Here I have his estimate: between April and July
Sixty-one deaths suffered in old age
But an old age of forced labour, their backs bent twice,
Under the weight of years and under the mule-whip.
Also thirty-eight deaths of healthy men
Who made some show of reluctance or momentary
Impatience.

  Moses.   That was a good cure. They are now
Patient for all eternity.

Aaron. Also the deaths
Of seven pregnant women, forced to dig
Until they had become their own gravediggers.
Also the deaths of nineteen children, twelve
Unofficial crucifixions...

Seti. This is intolerable
Singsong! Am I to compose the epitaphs
For every individual grave of this trying summer?
I have my figures. I do not need yours.

Moses. Twelve hundred thousand. These are the men
I have come to find. They are the wound in my mind.
They show me myself covered in blood: and you
Are there, staring back at yourself from that mortal
Mirror, twelve hundred thousand times yourself,
Which, like a dog with its own reflection,
You don't recognize. No recollection?
Not of this child, elect in its private maze?
Not of this boy rashly making manhood
Out of a clumsy alteration? Is this some other
Form of life than yours? What; is nothing like?
The girls dandling to-morrow, the young men
Trying to justify to-day, old men
Sitting by monuments of memory—
All these licking their fingers of experience
To turn the page.—No! I am mistaken.
They are only pestilence-carriers and tomb makers.
But the worst pestilence they carry is the cruelty
Of Pharaoh. That is what I have come to show you.

Seti. Very well; you have introduced yourself;
I have understood you. Is it not a pity
That you had taken up this attitude
Before you were aware of mine? I can see
How, knowing, as you must, your own capabilities,

You would fill those listless hours of your exile
With dreams of action. Action is what I have for you.
But there's a whiff of anarchy about you.
You cannot hope that I should like it. A generalship—
The confidence of Egypt—these do not look well
On an agitator. Something has to go.—
I have put men to a purpose who otherwise
Would have had not the least meaning.

  Moses.   Aaron,
What am I doing fitting one word against another
To see them melt as soon as they touch this man?
Not the least meaning, except the meaning
Of the breath in your lungs, the mystery of existing
At all. What have we approached or conceived
When we have conquered and built a world? Even
Though civilisation became perfect? What then?
We have only put a crown on the skeleton.
It is the individual man
In his individual freedom who can mature
With his warm spirit the unripe world.
What would you make of man? If you diminish him
To a count of labouring limbs, you also will dwindle
And be an unmeaning body, decomposing
Imperceptibly under heavy ornaments.
They are your likeness, these men, even to nightmares.
I have business with Egypt, one more victory for her,
A better one than Ethiopia:
That she should come to see her own shame
And discover justice for my people.

  Seti. You have fermented in your Midian bottle.
But lately I have learnt an obstinate patience.
We should have done better to have met
Out of the sun. We can do better than this

And so we shall yet, later, at a cooler time.
Where will you sleep? We will see you have food.
Do you remember, I wonder, the palace nectarine?

(MOSES *and* AARON *go towards the steps*)

I said, where will you lodge?
Moses.   With my sister, Miriam.
Seti (to ANATH). Do you know where that is?
Anath.   Perfectly.
Seti (going in).   Very well.
Anath. Now he will not sleep again tonight.
Moses. I hope that none of us will sleep again
Until we all can sleep.
Anath.   And so once more
We see each other. You have chosen a fine day.

(MOSES *waits.* ANATH *says no more. He goes with* AARON)

Anath. I taught him to walk, Ramases. I also taught him
To speak and say his alphabet. I taught you your
Alphabet also; and also Teusret hers.
I have been a really useful woman.
Ramases.   Where
Does his sister live?
Anath.   Why do you want to know?
Ramases. I wondered where it might be.
Anath.   She has a tent
By the brick-kiln.
Ramases.   We used to ride that way
And leave presents on a woman there. Was that
The sister?
Anath.   Yes; Miriam. His sister Miriam.
Ramases, let what has happened work itself out.
Don't finger it. Do you hear me?
Ramases.   I liked that man.

Anath. So have others before you. Do not finger it.
Your father is not always quite at his best.
  Ramases. I know my father.
  Anath.   Maybe.
  Ramases.   I seem to love him.
  Anath. You should.
  Ramases.   And yet I could like that man.
  Anath. Well, like that man; but do not raise a hand
To help that man; do not sing with that man
Or let him make his nest in your brain. Like him,
Ramases, forget him, and let us live in peace.
  Ramases. I shall go and find him.
  Anath.   Ramases, come here.
Do you want to make yourself look like a laughable puppy
Bounding after his heels? Stay where you are.
I ask it of you. I ask you to put him from your mind.
Do you hear? I ask you to forget him.
  Ramases.   How?
  Anath. What would make it difficult?
  Ramases.   Can you forget him?
  Anath. He has gone.
  Ramases.   And something of us, I think, went with him.
  Anath. Well, you will let him go. I have asked you.
  Ramases.   No.
I love you, you know that. But trust me a little.
I shall be discreet.   (*Exit* RAMASES)
  Anath.   Ramases!—No,
What should I be doing, turning his feet
Towards my fears? (*She goes to the parapet*)
             I guess at a reticent power
Above the days of our life.
Our most convinced actions are only questions,
And the power will answer as it wishes.

If I do not act, it will still answer.
But it will not have been my question.

(Enter TEUSRET)

Teusret.   Aunt Anath—
Anath.   Do you remember, Teusret?
A man fell from the pyramid—only this morning.

CURTAIN

SCENE TWO

MIRIAM'S *tent.*   MOSES *(in the entrance).*   MIRIAM.

Moses. Miriam! Miriam!
Miriam.   Is it my brother? Yes;
You have his immovable look. Aaron told me
To expect you.
Moses.   Can you be Miriam?
Miriam.   A kind
Of residue. Sit down, if you don't mind.
I dislike answering questions. Ask me nothing.
I am very well; I have nothing to offer you
To drink.
Moses.   I'm glad to be with you after so long.
Miriam.   You will find it very tiresome after five or six minutes.
I repeat myself unendurably, like the Creation.
Your only hope is to deaden yourself to me
And it.
Aaron (in the entrance).   Your name runs like fire, like an ostrich!
You didn't wait to hear, but the sergeant at the gate
Is full of it. They've started campaigns of gossip
And altercation in the assembly-gardens—
As soon as this; before you've even been seen!
Moses. And what will this do for us?

Aaron.   Surely it suggests
They're taking sides? It was noticed a minister's wife
Was wearing an M in small lilies; her daughter snatched them off
And threw them among the pigeons. How can Seti
Assure himself what size your faction is?
Egypt loves and hates you inextricably.

Moses. Egypt is afraid. Love me? No;
They're afraid to be without me.

Aaron. That will pass for love.

Moses. They love me from the bottom of their greed.
Give me the bad news. What men have we lost?

Miriam. So you're not only here on a visit to your sister.

Aaron. Here is a list. It's not complete.

Miriam.   I've had
Enough of trouble.

Moses.   Rahnor, Janeth, Pathrusim—
Is he lost? Pathrusim? The sand of Egypt
Is abominably the richer.—Hadoram, Seth,
Havilah, Dodanim...

Miriam.   Why do you read
Dead men's names? There are some of us still breathing.
Your sister, for example, is still alive,
Figuratively speaking. I imagined
You would have plenty to tell me. Have you not?
Am I always to know nothing of you?

Moses.   These names are what I am.

Miriam. They are yesterday's life. I liked many of them very well;
But we no longer have anything in common.

Aaron. Are we to forget them because we have lost them?

Miriam.   To wish
To be with them comes too easily.

Moses.   This tent
Is stifling.

Miriam. I keep it closed. I have no liking
For what goes on outside.

  Moses.   When do they say
The mountains last had rain?

  Miriam.   Nine months ago.

  Moses. It's time for parturition.
Look: what you shut out is a withering city.
City of Egypt. This land once I worshipped,
And now I cannot be sure what I bring against her
In my heart. This noon, like every other noon,
Still groans with the laborious wheels which drew
The Nile water. There is little difference
Between ourselves and those blindfolded oxen.
We also do the thing we cannot see,
Hearing the creaking pivot and only knowing
That we labour.

  Miriam. Why did you bring him? Take yourselves off!
This is my tent, and it's not for restless hands.
He's a dangermaker still. Only watch his hands!

  Aaron. What has he said, Miriam?

  Miriam.   I have a son
And that is all I rest on. There's a man
Who should have been my brother. A king's daughter
Swallowed him and spat out this outlaw. I'll
Not have any more in the family.

  Aaron.   What should make them?

  Miriam. You and he. I know. Two years ago
I had it all: the surly men coming in here,
One at a time by signal, hardly nodding
Towards me, covering the table with their knife-cuts
To show how revolution must come, and freedom,
And idiocy; till a beetle striking the lamp
Or the coal settling, would shiver through us all

As though a dagger had sung into the pole.
And Espah and Zoad are dead from it. And you
In a night of loud hyenas went over the border.
Not again. I'll keep my nights of sleep, and I'll keep
My son.

   Aaron. In this country of murder?

   Miriam.   I'll keep my son
In whatever country.

   Moses.   Happily?

   Miriam.   We have
A way of living. We have the habit. Well?
It becomes a kind of pleasantness.

   Moses.   You have gone
With the dead after all, but you pretend not to see them.
Miriam, we have to speak to them with our lives.
Death was their question to us, and our lives
Become their understanding or perplexity.
And by living to answer them, we also answer
Our own impermanence. But this rule of Egypt
Denies us life, Miriam, and gives us nothing
With which we can outspeak our graves.

   Miriam.   I am angry;
The pity is I am angry. I must pretend
You have said nothing.

   Aaron.   But do you understand him?
In fact, do I understand him?

   Miriam.   In fact, do we need to?
I've no doubt he is kind, but not our kind. Very well,
I will say something. I'll say he's a sightseer;
And we keep our experience.

   Moses.   When I was a child,
Miriam, and you came like comfort to the huge
Nursery of the Pharaohs, we'd go hand

In hand along your stories, Hebrew stories
Which like contraband you put quietly in
To become my nature. What have you for me now?

Miriam. How she disliked me then! But what a talent
For condescension she had. I never saw you
After you were a child except by waiting
Among the crowd in the streets. There was no need
To come from Midian to tell me what my life is;
I have a bowing acquaintance with it. I knew it
When I hid you to save you from the knives.
Before I could talk it talked to me
In most difficult words.

Moses.   What words, Miriam?

Miriam. Pogrom, for one. And the curses of children
When I ran towards them expecting to play.
We have a wildfowl quality of blood,
Moses, temptation for sportsmen.

Moses.   Go on.

Miriam.   With what
If you please? Do you know the secret which will change
Our spoor? Our grandfather was stoned. I imagine
Creation tried our blood, and brought it in guilty.

Moses. It was the verdict of Chaos.

Miriam.   The thick of Chaos
Can still be smelt in the air, then. It was never
Properly resolved.

Moses.   And I believed
I had strength!

Miriam.   Your quarrel is with what things are.

Moses. Above all, with what I am, the inconsiderable
Life, born of such distances of suffering
And experiences, such an orgasm of mankind,
Such hewing of a foothold in the rockface

Of darkness, such aeons of cause and purport,
Jets and flares of a vision and the blaze
Of undecipherable fury, ages
Of moons rising into airs of sleep,
Of suns relenting down into the hills
Away from triumph, beyond defeat—and yet
My spirit, fruit of these life-throes of time,
Paces the condemned cell, the human body,
Incapable, weaponless, fettered with flesh, drinking
The moisture of the walls. Is the spirit
So masterly, that nature must obstruct it
Or be consumed? I feel it. Oh, it points!
I am there, beyond myself, if I could reach
To where I am. Miriam, you have shown me too much.

Miriam. One grows accustomed.

Aaron.   You will find the approach
And the means you want, I'm confident. Something
Will soon open a way to action.

Ramases (in the tent-opening).   Uncle.
I knew you as that. When I have thought of you
It has been as my uncle. You may not like it.
You may not want to see me, even.

Miriam.   The palace!

Aaron. Well, why not? Another man has been royal
And is here.

Miriam.   Has been, has been.

Ramases.   Moses.

Moses. Welcome and unwelcome.

Ramases.   I haven't come
From my father. I used schoolboy's worship, like myrrh
And cassia, with gums of memory,
To perpetuate you: the immense and affable
God in general's uniform, who came

And went between wars, who filled the schoolroom; and I
Could call him uncle. So when the memory
Broke its wrappings, and stood speaking like a man
On a noonday terrace, I decided to come nearer.

  Moses. Come on, then, and send the god to vanish finally
Into the lie that he always was.

  Ramases.   You spoke
To my father too suddenly.

  Moses.   Yes, we're precipitous,
We gods. We threw off the world, vegetable
And animal too, on the impulse of an imaginative
Moment. But we lost interest.

  Ramases.   You mean
I'm a boy to you still.

  Moses.   You came by your boyhood honestly.
Mine I stole. I had no right to it.

  Aaron.   Why
Do you turn him away, Moses? Why not talk to him?

  Moses. What would we talk of, Aaron? What quiet subject?
They tell me centuries of horror brood
In this vivid kingdom of fertile mud. Do you think
If we swung the rattle of conversation
Those centuries would fly off like so many crows?
They would wheel above us and come to feed again.

  Aaron. But what do you think of? I sometimes call you, to myself,
A gate without a key. You'll open when you will.
Such a gate must lead somewhere, so I believe,
Though perhaps that sounds fanciful. Where shall we find a better
Opportunity?

  Ramases.   I have my father mapped
So that I know which way to travel. Listen,
Uncle—he says he would have recalled you, which means
He needs you here. He'll be friendly if you let him.

I kept a buckle of your uniform—this one, the lion-head.
Take it again, take our army and be our general.
You'll become inseparable from Egypt's safety;
Then he will listen. Then you can direct
His goodwill past yourself to these Israelites.

Aaron. It's true. You have the buckle, and we're agreed, then.
My dreams were less; not a third as felicitous.

Moses. Egypt and Israel both in me together!
How would that be managed? I should wolf
Myself to keep myself nourished. I could play
With wars, oh God, very pleasantly. You know
I prosper in a cloud of dust—you're wise
To offer me that. And Egypt would still be,
In spite of my fathers, a sufficient cause.

Aaron. Yes, it would be sufficient.

Moses.   Splendid, then.
What armour shall I wear? What ancestral metal
Above my heart? Rib, thighbone and skull:
Bones from the mines of Egypt. I will clank
To Egypt's victory in Israel's bones.
Does this please you? Does it not? Admire
How when preparing a campaign I become
Oblivious to day and night, and in
The action, obsessed. How will that do? I make
My future, put glory into Egypt, enjoy myself
Into your father's confidence—yes, that,
I know; and being there, perhaps I coax
Little concessions for the Hebrew cause
To justify me.—Idiot, idiot!
I should have lost them, Aaron, and be lost,
More than when in Midian I sat
Over my food and let them trudge in my bowels.

Aaron. I have faith in your judgment. Nevertheless, this is

Something to be thought of, a reality of a kind.

Moses. Like adultery.

Miriam.   Offer of a generalship?
Of course I don't understand. But like adultery?
To be a general? Do you mean us to think
You would refuse—

Moses.   You both would like to see
Your brother fat, but your brother has a fancy
To be as lean as Israel.

Miriam.   Where do you see
Israel now?

Moses.   Where do I see God?
Be certain, Israel is. I am here to be a stone
In her sling, out of her gall.

Ramases.   Will you promise to be patient?
There will be difficulties to be got over;
I have a father. But at some future time
When I am Pharaoh—

Moses.   By then I may be free
To let my bones talk of their disinterest
In the world's affairs: and whether it is Hebrew
Or Egyptian, man will cry for me no longer.

Miriam. Listen!

Aaron.   What is it?

Miriam.   Nothing, nothing—I imagined—
Why should he be back at this time? What
Could bring him now? Listen!

Moses.   What do you hear?

Miriam. It's the whistle he gives when he's reaching home.

Aaron.   Her son.
It's Shendi.

Miriam. Something has happened. The negro lynx
Was in my sleep last night praying to become

A man, but only dead birds came out of its mouth.
Why is the palace here? What are you doing here
In my home? He cannot even come home.

Ramases.   Is this
Egypt?

Miriam. Do you hear him again? No nearer, no nearer.
He is being prevented. Can I get to him
Without being seen? Stay where you are. No one
Must see me, no one.

(*She goes out. In a moment* A A R O N *follows her*)

Ramases.   You all think of me
As an enemy.

Moses.   We're not enemies so much
As creatures of division. You and I,
Ramases, like money in a purse,
Ring together only to be spent
For different reasons.

Ramases.   Different? How am I
To be spent, then?

Moses.   How? Why, upon solids,
On heritage, the one thing positive.
Our roots are the element which gives us purpose
And life. There will be summers to come which need
The lotus. That will be for you.

Ramases.   So let
The lotus stink. Am I never to see you?

Moses.   No,
It would be better, never. Forget me, Ramases.

Ramases. That anyway is impossible. I know
I bear your mark, and how will you obliterate
That? Do you forget the feel of the year
When you were as I am? They count me as a man,
Just. But the boy is still in my head and mouth.

I feel him there. I speak him. I should burn
Throne and lotus gladly if I could break
Myself of boyhood, if burning would do it. But you
Are clear and risen roundly over the hazes.
You have the formula. I need it.

Moses.   Clear?
Evidence of that! Where in this drouthy
Overwatered world can you find me clarity?
What spirit made the hawk? a bird obedient
To grace, a bright lash on the cheek of the wind
And drawn and ringed with feathered earth and sun,
An achievement of eternity's birdsmith. But did he
Also bleak the glittering charcoal of the eyes
And sharpen beak and claws on his hone of lust?
What language is life? Not one I know.
A quarrel in God's nature. But you, at least,
Are pronounceable: heir of Egypt, heir of Egypt.
That is yourself.

Ramases.   You mean I'm of no value
Except to be Egypt's ornament.

Moses.   Of much
Value; infinite.

Ramases.   But we stay unfriendly?

Moses. Because I taste your boyhood and remember mine
And like them both.

Ramases.   But even so—

Moses.   You shall stay as you are.

Ramases. Exactly as I am, a friend of Moses.

Moses. They're coming with Shendi. Keep with me in the shadow.

(*Enter* MIRIAM *and* AARON, *supporting* SHENDI)

Miriam. He has been so strong. Are you ill? How are you ill?
You can speak, surely you can speak? We don't know them;

That's what is worst—our own—even in childhood
They say so little.

  Aaron.   Lie here, Shendi.

  Miriam.   Still
And quiet. What shall I do for him? They're ourselves
But quite dark to us. Things happen without warning.

  Aaron. Give him this water.

  Miriam.   A sip, and then you shall have more.
My fingers are hot. I must drench my hands. Aaron,
We have been unhappy. What can we do with water?
A sip again. I feel your heart in your forehead.

  Shendi. They'll come.

  Miriam.   Keep yourself quiet.

  Shendi.   Yes, they will come,
They'll come for me, they'll find me!

  Aaron.   What have you done?

  Miriam. Done?

  Shendi.   What are you holding me for? Must I always
Be held? It was the sun! Don't you know that?
They make madmen in the sun. Thousands of madmen
Have been made in the sun. They say nothing, nothing at all,
But suddenly they're running—no, not they,
It's only their bodies that are running: the madmen
Are still standing in the sun, watching their bodies
Run away. Can they kill me for that? Or what, or what?
It was the strike that made it happen!

  Aaron.   What have you said?
What strike?

  Miriam.   He's ill!

  Shendi.   No, it was the sun; not the strike,
The sun. The noise of the strike, the whips.

  Aaron.   The strike?
What was it? What has happened?

Shendi.   The spermy bastards!
They make us hit the earth like spit.
  Miriam.   What are you saying?
Don't ask him any more!
  Aaron.   I'll make him tell me. What strike?
What has happened?
  Shendi.   I don't know what has happened.
The brickmakers began it. A youngster was with me,
Twelve years old, and he left me to watch the trouble.
I saw them take him away, they dragged him off
To the captain at the gate, because he was watching.
It has nothing to do with it. It's the sun. Have you heard
The order? They'll not give us straw to make the bricks;
We must gather the straw ourselves; but the tale of bricks
Must be more, more! What does it matter? Who says
It matters? They're coming for me.
  Miriam.   It cannot happen,
Shendi, it cannot.
  Moses.   Cannot happen, cannot be.
Cannot. Earth, life, ourselves are impossibility;
Impossible even as lie or legend. What is this Pharaoh
Who answers me with this? Does he hope
To make himself exist? Tell him it isn't possible.
Existence is beyond conception.
  Shendi.   Who's that?
My uncle, is it? The great fellow that was.
The man who thought he was Egypt. Have you come
To try again, murderer? Look at your crop of relations
And how they do in the land you dunged for us.
Never mind. You did very well.—Oh, what will happen?
Do you hear that? They're whipping the side of the tent.
You know I can't stand up, they've come for me,
You know it was the sun—uncle, uncle!

Miriam. It was neighbours talking, it was only the neighbours.

                                                        —Aaron,
It was neighbours talking. Wasn't it, wasn't it?

                    (*Enter* TWO OVERSEERS)
                                                  No, no!

1st Overseer. Nice family. Here's the man we want.

2nd Overseer.   Get up,
Little rat. So you'd strike? We'll teach you striking.
Striking's our specialty. Eh? Not bad! We'll strike him!

Miriam. He's sick—can't you see?

1st Overseer.   That's enough of that.

Ramases.   What is this?
Weren't you told I had sent for him?

2nd Overseer.   My crimes!

Ramases. Well, weren't you told?

1st Overseer.   No, sir; no, your holiness; not told.
I beg pardon, sir. I didn't see you, my lord, didn't see you.

Ramases. I tell you now. I sent for him. Go away.

1st Overseer. Yes, lord.

2nd Overseer.   Yes, almighty.

                              (*They back away out of sight*)

Miriam. You're here, Shendi, you're here. The prince has kept you.
He spoke for you. Forgive me, I'm more afraid than ever.
Forgive me. Relief is very like an illness.

Shendi. No one warned—What are you doing with me?
Is it a trick? What did I say before they came?
My lord, I was ill. I don't know what is happening.

Ramases. Nothing is happening. You can rest.

Aaron.   For us
Much is happening. I begin to have hope.
Eh, Moses? This is the boy who will be our man,
The palace key. In the belly of our misfortune
We find our hope.

Moses.   We're not ready to hope
Or to despair; not ready to doubt or to believe.
We're equipped to do no more than confront ourselves.
And if we were equipped for more, hoping
Or despairing, I wouldn't use him. My need is something
Different: I need to know how good
Can be strong enough to break out of the possessing
Arms of evil: good, rectitude,
The popular song, whistled by the world in the streets;
And evil whistles the same air back again.
Gigantic, mastering evil! And what we accept
As good, breaks it less than the incision of wheat
Breaks the ground. Where shall I look for triumph?
Somewhere, not beyond our scope, is a power
Participating, but unharnessed, waiting
To be led towards us. Good has a singular strength
Not known to evil; and I, an ambitious heart
Needing interpretation. But not through this boy,
Never through this boy. I will not use him!

CURTAIN

SCENE THREE

A room in the Palace, giving on to the terrace of Scene One. ANATH *is standing on the terrace.* TEUSRET'S *voice is heard calling "Ramases! Ramases!" It draws nearer.* ANATH *comes into the room and listens for* TEUSRET'S *voice which now comes from farther away. She turns to go back to the terrace. Enter* RAMASES.

Anath. Have you seen him?
Ramases.   Moses?
Anath.   Have you seen your father?

Ramases. He made me a present of my future, with the royal seal
Attached. Did you know?

Anath.   I have to wish you happiness.
Dear, be happy. There's nothing better to be looked for.
Happiness is sometimes hard to recognize.
It seems so to keep company with the unlikely.
Teusret is looking for you.

Ramases.   Where is she?

Anath.   Everywhere.
Put your hand in one place, she is already
Beating her wings in another.

Ramases.   Listen—look—
What is it, this that has captured me? This "now",
This exact truth of time—certainly truth—
The moment we're now crossing. Can this truth
Vanish? Look, your shadow thrown over the chair,
That dog's jerking bark, the distance of whistling,
A gate clanging-to, the water thrown into the yard,
Your fingers travelling your bracelet, my voice—listen,
My voice—your breathing—

               (TEUSRET *is heard calling* RAMASES)

               And Teusret running through the empty rooms.
It is true for us now, but not till now, and never
To be again. I want it for myself.
This is my life.

               (*Enter* TEUSRET)

            It has gone.

Teusret.   I've found you at last.
Where have you been hidden? Where were you?

Ramases.   With father.

Teusret. For an hour!
No one could tell me. The rooms were all deserted.

Just as it happens in my sleep sometimes; but then
The door on the other side of the room is always
Closing behind you, and the room is empty—I never
Come to you.

  Ramases.   But, awake, it's different. You find me.

  Teusret. Why did he talk for so long?

  Ramases.   I'm to be married
He says.

  Teusret. I had a riddle to ask you. Fareti
Taught it to me.

  Ramases.   What is it?

  Teusret.   Ramases,
When will you be married?

  Ramases.   Soon, he says.

  Teusret. Why? Why? You can't! What does he mean?
Then—if you did—Why have you said so? Oh,
Why did you say it?

  Ramases.   Teusret—

  Teusret.   Who is it?

  Ramases.   The Syrian.
Her name is Phipa.

  Teusret.   Do you think that's pretty?
Phipa, Phipa, Phipa! The noise a flute makes
When the mouth's too full of saliva. You won't do it.

  Ramases. What can I say?

  Anath.   Teusret, we all, you will find,
Belong to Egypt: our lives go on the loom
And our land weaves. And the gods know we need
Some such alliance. If the dynasty is safe
We can at least be partly ourselves. He will need
Both of us still.

  Teusret.   He won't. He will be changed.
The days will be different and I shall be the same.

How shall I be happy then?

(*Enter* SETI)

Will *you* be?

Are you glad?

Seti.   Can you imagine, Teusret,
The frantic compulsion which first fetched man forming
And breathing out of the earth's dust? Such
A compulsion of beauty has this Phipa of Syria,
With the addition of wit and a good head for business.
She's immensely rich. Homegoing sailors,
When there are no stars, steer perfectly for Syria
Merely by thinking of her. So they say.
A figure of her, hung under the bows
And kissing the wake, ensures a harvest of fish.

Teusret.   What a tale!

Seti.   Well, yes, but she has beauty.

Teusret.   Flowers for Ramases
Then! We must make it an occasion. I'll fetch my lute
And celebrate. Garlands! I'll make you into
A nice little afternoon god. Don't go away.

Ramases. Here, Teusret—

Teusret.   You have earned a ceremony.
Would you rather have me in tears? This isn't silliness
But a proper formality. I need to do it.
Wait here, all of you.   (*Exit* TEUSRET)

Anath.   Let her do what she must.

Ramases (*sings*). "If under my window
The dark will not lose me
No one will see me a maiden again." Father,
I have something to ask you. It has to do with Moses.

Seti. He needn't trouble you.

Ramases.   Nor any of us. But haven't you
Overlooked his nephew?

Seti.   This is nothing to you.
Nothing to you at all.
  Ramases.   Nothing at all.
Moses has a sister and a nephew.
The nephew's a labourer. Might there not here be a way
By which you could come at Moses?
  Seti.   Statesmanship,
My son, is the gods' gift to restrain their own
Infidelities to man. As for Moses,
I'll comprehend him when he's comprehensible.
  Ramases. Such as a commission for this nephew; or a place in the palace.
Or whatever you consider is best. What would you wish?
What do you say? Can you talk of honours
To a man whose family is unhonoured? I don't know,
But you will know.
  Seti.   Who told you to speak of him?
What do you know of this name that you're bandying? Anath?
You have stared enough at that pyramid. Is this
Your influence?
  Anath.   Am I a planet, to be
So influential? No, Seti; it is not.
I would rather infect him with something less dubious
Than the blood of Moses.
                    (*Enter* TEUSRET *with a lute and flowers*)
  Teusret.   Look, I have them. I got them
Out of my room. They were round my bronze Isis.
Shall I have offended her?
  Seti.   Do you know this nephew?
  Anath. I've seen him.
  Seti.   How did he promise?
  Anath.   He promised to be male,
As though he might have the ability for a beard
I thought.

Teusret.   Are you all ready for the ceremony?
Ramases, you must be in a chair; this chair.
  Ramases. Can it be tried?
  Seti.   What is it now?
  Ramases.   To mark
My coming of age. May I commission the nephew?
  Seti. That is still to be known. I must have precise
Information of him. Now forget the question.
The window on the east side of your room
Is the window that looks toward Syria.
  Teusret.   Why must you go
Before you see Ramases in flowers? And when
Have you ever heard me play on my lute?   (*Exit* SETI)
                              Has no one
Told him he has a daughter?
  Anath.   The flowers were schooled
With salamanders, to be so enduring
In this furnace.
  Ramases.   Will he really do it?
  Anath.   The land
Is rocking, remember. He'll take hold even of grass.
  Teusret. Let me begin. Neither of you has any sense
Of occasion. These on your shoulders. What *are* flowers?
What is the bridge to be crossed, I wonder,
From a petal to being a wing or a hand? These
For your brows. Does the scent of them sicken you?
My pollen fingers.
  Ramases.   They're shattering already.
  Teusret. Some of them are too full.
  Ramases.   You've brought me the garden.
Here's an earwig on my hand.
  Teusret.   Tread on it. Now
You're ripe to receive a god. Isn't he, Aunt?

Does he look noble? My brother in bloom.

Ramases (*treading on the earwig*). Out goes he. Let's get your singing
  over.

Teusret (*staring*). I have to remember you. Sing with me.

Anath.   I?

Sing? With the crack in my voice? Not songs for bridegrooms.
Only songs in the minor, where a false note
Can be taken to be excessive sensibility.

Teusret. Nothing, nothing will go on in the old way.
I wonder, can I remember which is the key? (*She touches the lute*)

Ramases. Did you know my father had ordered the Israelites
To gather their own straw?

Anath.   Yes, I knew.

Ramases.   Why did he?

Anath. A little show of invulnerability.

Ramases. Is Moses safe here?

Teusret.   I wish there were echoes in this room,
A choir of them, to be company for my voice.
You will have to help me when I lose myself.

(*Sings*)   Why should there be two
                      Where one will do,
                Step over this shadow and tell me
                    And my heart will make a ring
                        Sighing in a circle
                And my hands will beckon and bring
                    The maiden fortune who befell me
                        O fortune, fortune.
                      (*Enter* Seti)

You see, father,—doesn't he look married already?

(*Sings*)   Why do we breathe and wait
                      So separate?
                The whirl in the shell and the sand
                    Is time going home to time

Kissing to a darkness.
So shall we go, so shall we seem
In the gardens, hand in hand.
O fortune, fortune.

So changed against the sun—

(She is interrupted by MOSES, *who enters bearing in his arms a dead Israelite boy)*

Anath. What are we to have now?

Ramases.   The wrong of a right.

Seti. What is this? Isn't it enough that you broke
Into Egypt unasked but you must—

Moses.   This is your property.
Of little value. Shall I bury it in your garden?
You need have no anxiety. It will not grow.

Anath. Oh, in the name of the gods—

Seti.   Is your reason gone?

Moses (laying the body at SETI's *feet).* Look: worthless, worthless.
    The music needn't stop.
You killed him.

Seti.   As I thought; you've let your brain
Suffer in this heat. I saw, in the first few words
You spoke this morning, it would end in this.

Teusret. Ramases!

Seti.   You frighten children, you see.
It's too ambitious.

Teusret.   That boy!

Ramases.   That isn't death
Lying on the ground.

Teusret.   It is! It is! It is!

Seti. Well? Tell me: is it an act of sanity
To carry this child here? I'm sorry to see it.

Take him and have him buried. You know it wasn't
Done by me.

   Moses.   It was done of you. You'll not
Escape from yourself through the narrows between By and Of.
Your captain killed him on the metal of your gates, as with
A score of others. If it wasn't done of you
Fetch the captain, condemn him to death, and watch
How he'll stare.

   Seti.   I'll see the man. It's understood.

   Moses. Who understands? And what is understood?
If you move your foot only a little forward
Your toe will be against your power. Is this
How you imagined your strength to be—ungrowing,
Unbreathing, a child, and dead? Out of him
Comes your army, your fleet, the cliff of gold
You move on, pride, place, adulation
And name—out of this contemptible chrysalis—
Not this, not even this, but this destroyed,
This refused to itself. Fetch in your captain,
Fetch in your thousand captains, and condemn them
For the murder of your power.

   Seti.   What would I give
To see you for a moment with your old grasp
And intelligence. Nature, you may remember,
Is lavish, and in return for being understood,
Not hoarded, gives us civilisation.
Would you have the earth never see purple
Because the murex dies? Blame, dear Moses,
The gods for their creative plan which is
Not to count the cost but enormously
To bring about.

   Moses.   And so they bring about
The enormity of Egypt. Is that the full

Ambition of your gods? Egypt is only
One golden eruption of time, one flying spark
Attempting the ultimate fire. But who can say
What secrets my race has, what unworked seams
Of consciousness in mind and soul? Deny
Life to itself and life will harness and ride you
To its purpose. My people shall become themselves,
By reason of their own god who speaks within them.
What I ask is that I may lead them peaceably
Into the wilderness for a space, to find
Their god and so become living men at last.

  Seti.   More favours, something new. What god is this?

  Moses.   The inimitable patience who doesn't yet
Strike you down.

  Seti.   He and I have something in common
If he has patience. Shall I plough your madness
And sow what I can of perception, or is the ground
Too arid with your envy? My trust is Egypt
And the maturity of the world. Where should I look
For my worth, if I plunged my hand into the body
Of the kingdom, and with a pale flower smell of humanity
Released each bone and blessed each nerve and drop
Of blood and left them to the elements?
Or, gathering them in again when each by the wonder
Of its individual god had learnt a new
Desire of life, put them with their untutored
Ambitions back to the corporate achievement,
To watch their incoherence? Where then
Is the painfully acquired stature and beauty
Of mankind?

  Moses.   Where is it now? Your stature and beauty
Is an untarred fleet which the waves rot while it rides them.
You know well enough the dark places of the fish

Under your palace floor: invasion is probable,
Unrest is in and out of doors, your southern half
Splits from the north, the lords at your table
Are looking down at their hands. And flowing through all
Is the misery of my blood. Let that be clean
First, and then the flesh may heal.

   Seti.   Your god
Has already taken your senses into his bosom;
No doubt he'll fetch your race to join them. But I
Can't laugh. The public ear goes too easily
To bed with lies. I have nursed you enough.
Now dungeons can nurse you. Your god can find you
Behind the walls and return your reason when he will.

   Anath. Seti! Are you sure? Will the surly half
Of Egypt believe he was mad?

   Seti.   Do you still play
At being his mother?

   Anath.   Do you think I do?
If you could see what my heart does, you could watch me
Destroying him.

   Moses.   If you destroy me, Seti,
Destruction will end with you.

   Ramases.   There could have been
Some other way than this. Is only Israel
Present to you, as once it was only Egypt?
Are you still Moses? Or who? Who are you?

   Anath. Does he know?

   Seti.   A man without laws.

   Moses.   What are the laws,
Other than those laws, stupendous and balancing,
Which made the hurl of smiting, infamous fires
Wheel in perfection, perpetually,
In great unaltering constellations:

The devotion in time and place and appearance,
Memory of the first unrolling of light:
At the centre of which are we, uncentred man,
Pointing in distraction at nothing but our existence.
What are the laws? Tell me, you taker of lives!
I am here by fury and the heart. Is that not
A law? I am here to appease the unconsummated
Resourceless dead, to join life to the living.
Is that not underwritten by nature? Is that
Not a law? Do not ask me why I do it!
I live. I do this thing. I was born this action.
Who can say for whom, for what ultimate region
Of life? A deed is what it becomes. And yet
What are the laws? Despite you, through you, upon you,
I am compelled.

(*A distant long cracking sound of thunder.* MOSES *jerks
back his head to listen*)

                    Are we overheard? Behind
The door that shuts us into life, there is
An ear.
  Anath. The mountains are breaking the drought at last!
  Moses. It is not as we suppose! We are the fools
Of sense and sight. What shall I believe?
What league have we, the human, with the greater
Than human? Nothing is as we suppose!
The stream of Israel's cause has surely turned
The wheel that contains us. Now, if only to make
Death excel, life shall live. Am I given the power
To do what I am?
  Anath.   Do what you are! Be unborn,
Or a name spoken savagely before I lived.
The power to do what you are is self-destruction.

Ask it, ask it then, demand it! Crave it!
Dispossess time of your white face. Be unborn,
Unexisting, even though in going
You take the world with you!
  Moses. Am I given the power?
What says the infinite eavesdropper?

(*From horizon to horizon the sky is beaten into thunder*)

CURTAIN TO ACT ONE

ACT TWO

SCENE ONE

MIRIAM's *tent, the evening of the same day.* MOSES. AARON.

Moses. Has something come between us, or into what
Back room of your mind have you gone? You watch each word
As it comes out of my mouth, but I cannot see
What you do with it after you have watched.
You've something to say.

    Aaron.   I have nothing.

    Moses.   Must we bring
Lights to each other?

    Aaron.   Why do you have to say this?

    Moses. The present is always falling behind me. I seem
To do what was done long ago, and yet I still
Must grope and pummel to bring it into being.
It's the switch of time on our flanks, to make us
Pull the heavy moment.—Look: I shall divide them
Into groups a hundred or a hundred and fifty strong,
Each with a man to lead them, one they can trust,
Such as this man you mention, Morshad—
And the man I spoke with this evening. Put them down.

    Aaron. Morshad and Zedeth. Yes, I have them.

    Moses.   And then
This morning's rioting, the man who started that,
Whatever his name is. Will they listen to him again?

              (AARON *goes to the tent-opening and looks out*)
He made his move too early, some few days
Too soon.

    Aaron. I thought I felt the earth quiver.

    Moses. What is he called?

Aaron.   The earth has moved. It stirred
Like an animal. Moses!

Moses.   The man has a name. Put him down.

Aaron. Something unnatural has come awake
Which should have slept until time was finished.
I haven't made this out of fear. Or what
Is fear? Is it this—uncoiling, unexampled!
Listen! Did you hear a roar? A building
Has collapsed. The dust is like a cloud, higher
Than the city. Will you see?

Moses.   We have something more to do
Than to listen to falling cities. The dust will settle
While we Hebrews die. Come on; give me the names.

Aaron. It's you, yourself! You see, it's yourself! I knew
It wasn't I! And this is why I couldn't
Answer you. You have gone under yourself,
Under yourself or wherever it is—as though
Your reasonable plans and normal behaviour
Were a deception covering something
Utterly different. Were you waiting for this—
This, outside—this obsessed appalling sunset?
You see, I'm to pieces. Why does this mean nothing to you?
Why won't you come and see it?

Moses.   The names, the names.

(MIRIAM *stands in the opening, with a pitcher*)

Miriam. All the water is blood.

Aaron.   Miriam! What is happening to the city?

Miriam. There's no water, no water. Nothing but blood.

Aaron. Then my fear has foundation. The sun has set
On truth altogether. The evening's a perjury!
Let none of us be duped by it.

Miriam.   Did you really
Believe the world? So did we all. The water

Is blood. The river floods it over the fields.
The wells stink of it.

  Aaron.   What are you saying?

  Miriam.   Go out then
And see it yourself. The men who were thirsty enough
To drink what came, are lying at the well-heads
Vomiting.

  Moses.   What men? Ours?

  Miriam.   Egyptians.

  Moses.   Miriam,
What have you there?

  Miriam.   I filled my pitcher. We all
Filled our pitchers, everyone, in spite of—
Do you think we believed it could happen to us? To them
Perhaps, something might happen; to the others but not
To ourselves.

  Moses (*bringing his hand out of the pitcher*). Not to ourselves. To the
    others.

  Miriam.   Your hand
Has water on it! It is water!

  Moses.   From which well
Was this drawn?

  Miriam.   Our own. Are we likely to use the Egyptians'?
But I saw it, we all saw it.

  Moses.   The sun this last hour
Has been that colour. Doesn't it at evening
Fall directly on our well?

  Miriam.   The sun? Are we
Talking about the sun? Tell me I'm lying
And look at my feet. We slopped in blood flooding
From the Nile. I saw the Egyptians who drank it.

  Moses.   The Nile.
The Egyptians! But this water came from our well

Not theirs —Was I waiting, Aaron? I was waiting
Without expectation. But surely, I already knew?
And you—did you guess, as well, that we are such a part
Of the whole, more than time made clear to us?
Such projects of the unending, here projected
Into passing actions? We with our five bare fingers
Have caused the strings of God to sound.
Creation's mutehead is dissolving, Aaron.
Our lives are being lived into our lives.
We are known!

   Miriam.   Do you think it was you who made the Egyptians
Vomit? We may as well all be mad. The world
Has a disease. Let me away from it, and from you,
And away from myself. Where is Shendi?

   Aaron.   What's this?
Isn't there confusion enough? Confusion I call it!
A contradiction of what we have always known
To be conclusive: an ugly and impossible
Mistake in nature. And you, you of all men,
Accept it, identify yourself with it. It must be
Denied. What has become of you since yesterday?
Is it not possible still to be plain men
Dealing with a plain situation? Must we see
Visions? You were an unchallengeable leader once.
That is the man I follow. A plain soldier.

   Miriam. Where can Shendi be?

   Moses. The plainest soldier is sworn to the service of riddles.
Our strategy is written on strange eternal paper.
We may decide to advance this way or that way
But we are lifted forward by a wind
And when it drops we see no more of the world.
Shall we live in mystery and yet
Conduct ourselves as though everything were known?

If, in battle upon the sea, we fought
As though on land, we should be more embroiled
With water than the enemy. Are we on sea
Or land, would you say?

  Aaron.   Sea? Land? For pity's sake
Stay with reality.

  Moses.   If I can penetrate
So far.

  Miriam. What will you do for us? Not as much
As sleep will do, if there is any way
We can come at sleep. Do you think that we
Can sink fear in that water in the pitcher?
Why hasn't Shendi come home yet? It's past his time.
He should have stayed here the rest of the day.
Will you let me out of this intolerable night?
Are we going to stand here for ever?

  Shendi (in the tent-opening).   Mother!

  Miriam.   Shendi,
Has nothing happened to you? Let me see you and be
Reassured. Were you harmed by what I saw?

  Shendi. What have you seen? Nothing happened? Everything!
We've stepped across to a new life. Where were we living?
It was the appearance, of course, the appearance of hell.
Nothing like it at all, except in our minds, our poor
Minds. I was going to make you try to guess,
But such an idea could never come at a guess.
Never; it couldn't. They've made me an officer!

  Miriam. I don't—understand what you mean.

  Shendi.   Your son! You see?
They've made him an officer. Like an Egyptian officer.
Like? I am one. We didn't know, that was all,
The world is perfectly fair, something to laugh at.
The ridiculous difference between me this morning

And now! They found I was better with head than hands.

Miriam. Shendi, did you come by way of the wells? Did you see them?

Shendi. I expect so. They say they're diseased. Can you imagine
How I felt when they took me by the arm and led me
Apart from the other men? I almost fought them.
I knew I was going.to be beaten—

Miriam.   Shendi, stop!
What are you saying?

Shendi.   Hell is done, done,
Done with, over!

Moses.   For you.

Miriam.   They would never do it.
But then to-night everything is to be believed.
Nothing has any truth and everything is true.

Aaron. I believe it. Perhaps you will think I'm gullible
But here is something recognizable and encouraging.
An evocation, if you like, of better things;
And, considering the Pharaoh, as a gesture a prodigy.
You've already achieved something, Moses,
And in a way—

Shendi.   *He* has achieved? Achieved what?
You didn't hear what they said to me. This has nothing
To do with my uncle. You have my uncle on the brain.

Aaron. I can see what you mean.

Shendi.   I report at the officer's quarters
In half an hour. I'll take some of my things
Along with me now. Has the world always been known
To spring such wonders, do you think? You're to live with me,
Mother, do you understand? Follow on later
And ask for the new officer. At the officers' quarters.
Have you something you can give me to wrap this linen in?
The Libyans have broken across the border and massacred
Two companies of the border regiment.

Aaron.   What?

A massacre? When was this?

Shendi.   I don't know when.

Where have you put my razor? Four hundred Egyptians

Killed, they say. They talked as though

I were already one of themselves. They say

There's also a rumour of revolution in the south.

Aaron. Moses, do you hear?

Shendi.   Where is my razor?

Miriam.   There.

Did you see the wells? I don't know what life's doing.

I don't know how we're to think.

Aaron.   Ambitiously.

These incidents all march our way. The Libyans

Over the border—revolution— Time

Is preparing for us with a timely unrest.

We came to Egypt at the perfect hour as it happens.

Shendi. That's enough of talk like that!

Miriam.   As it happens;

If we knew what happens. Shendi an officer!

Will this be what we want, at last? As the Nile

Happens into blood. Shendi an officer.

Shendi. And the officers' quarters, remember: comfort.

Miriam.   As massacre

And revolution happens. As to-morrow

Happens, whatever happens to-morrow.

Shendi.   Come on,

I must go.

Moses.   Refuse this commission.

Shendi.   What did you say?

Moses. Refuse this commission.

Miriam.   Refuse it?

Shendi.   Listen to that!

As my uncle happens, this is no surprise.
Only one of the family must rise
And glow in Egypt. We see the Hebrew sky
Must only bear one star, and at that a meteor
Which has fizzled. The rest of us can keep
Against the ground, our light withering
Into painful roots, and lose the whole damned world
Because Moses prefers it. But in spite of that,
In spite of that, generous brother of my mother,
We hope to live a little.

   Aaron.   As who does not?
The Pharaoh, I quite see, will have his motives.
But we can outmove motives to our advantage;
And here surely is a kind of proffered hand.

   Miriam. Why should he refuse? How could he refuse? He couldn't.
But who except you would say he should?

   Shendi.   It's clear
Why he says it. It was he who came back for recognition
And I have got it.

   Moses.   Make yourself live, then, Shendi;
But be sure it is life. The golden bear Success
Hugs a man close to its heart; and breaks his bones.
We come upon ourselves, as though we were chance,
Often by the most unwilling decisions.
Our maturities hide themselves from our wishes.
And where at last we touch our natures into life
Is at that drastic angle of experience
Where we divide from our natures. What have they said,
These Egyptians? Come with us and we'll treat you well.
Not, come with us and we will treat
You and your people well.

   Aaron.   They will come in time
Even to say that.

Shendi (*to* MOSES). This sounds well
Indeed, from you!
  Miriam.   Shendi is to be all
That he can become—all; and I say so,
I who made him. Am I to go on holding
The guilt for his unhappiness when opportunity
Offers to deliver me from it? Guilt it was,
And damnation, for giving him birth. This will let me loose!
  Shendi. Why do we listen to him? I know how to value
The first fairness I've known. If you think so little
Of being alive, uncle, you will find they're assembling
Spears to flash on Libya. Why not make something
Of that? The tradition is that, once upon a time,
You didn't know the meaning of apprehension
Or fear—back in those days when it was you
They treated well.
  Anath (*in the tent-opening*). Does he still not apprehend
Or fear?
  Shendi. Madam, madam—
  Anath.   What are you doing
To Egypt, Moses?
  Moses.   What have you come for?
  Anath.   You.
And have you really no fear? You are afraid
Of me, I think. Isn't it I who possess
That level of yourself which you are in torment
To see again? Can something you do not want
Be so great a relentless need? Not anything
Of me, but what I have of you. Your thoughts
Cannot accept me, but I am here. Oh,
Poor man, I am here!
  Moses. I'm stronger than memory.
  Anath.   It sucks the blood.

What are you doing to Egypt, Moses?

Moses.   What
Is Egypt doing to Egypt?

Anath.   Or Egypt to you.
You shall try your strength against memory the insect.
Come with me. I came by the old walks.
What have I seen? You shall come with me
And see it and tell me, and see the men and women
Bewildered in the doorways, for the name of their world
Has changed from home to horror. And is this
What you have in your heart for Egypt? Then favour me
And also have it in your eyes.

Moses.   But why
Do you come to me? To whose blood has the Nile
Turned? It isn't mine. Can it be the spilt blood
Of Israelites that is flowing back on Egypt?
Why come to me?

Anath.   He wants reason! Rationalize
The full moon and the howling dog. I have less
Inclination to be here than the dog has to howl.
If you come with me to Seti, he's ready to talk to you.

Moses. We've talked already.

Anath.   He'll let you take your Hebrews
To make their worship, or whatever you want of them,
On some conditions which he'll tell you.

Aaron.   Good.
Events are moving.

Moses.   If Seti is so ready,
Why did you make the walk through the ominous evening
To remind me that I'm in Egypt?

Anath.   Because he is sitting
Pressing his thumbs together, wedged inactive
In between his decision and pride. What it is

To have to do with men! They live too large.
Isn't it so, Miriam? I'm ready to take you.

  Moses. I'll come.

  Aaron.   This will be a great day for Israel.

  Miriam. My son has been made an officer.

  Anath.   I shall be glad
Not to be alone this time, with the earth
Wavering to a hint of doom. I suppose
There have to be powers of darkness, but they should keep
To the rules. The sky is lighter. The worst may be over.

  Moses. Aaron, you will come too.

  Aaron.   It has been easier
Than I should have thought possible this morning.

                  (*Exeunt* ANATH, MOSES *and* AARON)

  Shendi. What is this business the Pharaoh has with my uncle?

  Miriam. I mustn't think of Moses. Many things
I must be sure to keep my thoughts quite away from.
What is it we have to do? A dark mind
And he has followed that woman.

  Shendi. Will he try to stop my commission going through?

  Miriam. No, no, he's forgotten it.

  Shendi.   What does he matter, then?
I'm an officer!

  Miriam.   How could the water be blood, Shendi?

  Shendi. What?

  Miriam.   I'll put your things together for you.
How grand we shall be!

CURTAIN

SCENE TWO

A room in the Palace.   SETI.   ANATH.

Anath. Keep the window covered, Seti. The terrace
Crackles with dying locusts. I looked out.
I seemed to look within, on to myself,
When I stood there and looked out over Egypt.
The face of all this land is turned to the wall.
I looked out, and when I looked to the north I saw
Instead of quiet cattle, glutted jackals,
Not trees and pasture but vulture-bearing boughs
And fields which had been sown with hail. And looking
To the south I saw, like falling ashes after fire,
Death after thirst, death after hunger, death
After disease. And when I looked to the east
I saw an old woman ridding herself of lice;
And to the west, a man who had no meaning
Pushing thigh-deep through drifts of locusts.

Seti. Well; these things are finished.

Anath.   And what happens
Now? What will you do when the mourners have done
Wailing, and men look across the havoc of their fields
And the bones of their cattle and say: You did this,
What happens now?

Seti.   Why am I to be blamed
For all the elemental poisons that come up fungoid
Out of the damps and shadows which our existence
Moves in? Can I put peace into the furious
God—epilepsy of earthquake and eruption?
What am I but one of those you pity?

Anath. You tricked him, you tricked Moses, and not once
But seven times. First when I, against

All my self-warning, approached the unapproachable
And brought him to you. Didn't you make him promises
Then, and break them? And that night your promises
Plagued our ears with a croaking mockery,
With an unceasing frog-echo of those words
Which had meant nothing; with a plague of frogs!
A second time you made promises, and a third time
And a fourth: seven times you've broken them
While the stews of creation had their way with Egypt.

   Seti. You say this, concoct this legend; you have become
Infected with the venom that's against me.

   Anath. No, I've no venom. I've no more efficacy
Than a fishwife who has been made to breed against
Her will; and so I'm shrill and desperate.
No power against misery! That's what our lives add up to.
Our spacious affability, our subtle intelligence,
Our delicate consciousness of worlds beyond the world,
Our persuasive dignity when sacrificing to the gods,
Our bodies and our brains can all become
Slutted with lice between afternoon and evening.
You tricked him a second time, and that is what
You saw: sweet made foul. And then the third time
And we became the dungheap, the lusted of flies,
The desirable excretion. Our pleasantness was flyblown.

   Seti. I've suffered this once with Egypt—
   Anath.   You tricked Moses.
And what has come of it I would bring back to you
Until pity came out of you like blood to the knife,
Remembering how disease swept all the cattle,
How we could not sleep for intolerable lowing
Till daylight rounded up the herds of wolftorn
Death. You tricked him, and that feculent moment
Filthied our blood and made of us a nation

Loathsome with boils. You had stirred up the muck
Which the sweet gods thought fit to make us of
When they first formed man, the primal putrescence
We keep hidden under our thin dress of health.
What a pretty world, this world of filthmade kings!
When, after the sixth time, the hail came down,
I laughed. The hail was hard, metallic, cold
And clean, beating on us with the ferocity
Of brainbright anger. As cut diamonds, clean,
Clean, and fit to be beaten down by. When
It stamped out the gardens and cracked the skulls of birds
It bruised away the memory of vermin
And struck our faces fairly. If then, if only
Then our consciousness had gone clean out,
Or if then you had let these Israelites go with Moses,
We should not now so vainly
Shuffle our fingers in the dust to find
The name we once were known by. But you tricked
For the seventh time, and then the curse of the locusts
Strangled the whole air, the whole earth,
Devoured the last leaf of the old life
That we had sometime lived. The land is naked
To the bone, and men are naked beyond the bone,
Down to the barest nakedness which until now
Hope kept covered up. Now climb and sit
On the throne of this reality, and be
A king.
　Seti.　　Anath! These plagues were not my doing
And you know they were not. No man would say I caused them.
Only a woman with her mind hung
With a curtain of superstition would say so.
　Anath.　　　　　　　　　　　　I admit it.
I am superstitious. I have my terrors.

We are born too inexplicably out
Of one night's pleasure, and have too little security:
No more than a beating heart to keep us probable.
There must be other probabilities.
You tricked Moses after I had gone myself
To bring him to you, and what followed followed.
  Seti. It is true I made certain concessions to Moses
And reconsidered them. I was prepared
To let him have his way, if in return
He would use his great abilities to our advantage
But am I to have no kind of surety
That he'll return, after this godhunt of his?
I said to him Take the men but their wives and children
Must remain. And then I went further: I told him to take
Both men and women, but the children must stay. And at last
I only insisted on their cattle, since our cattle
Were dead. I'll not be panicked by this chain
Of black coincidence, which he with his genius
For generalship has taken advantage of.
He presumes upon the eternal because he has
No power to strike his bargain. I have not done
These things to Egypt. I'll not hear it be said.
  Anath. Well, they're done. Blame has no value anyway.
There's not one of us whose life doesn't make mischief
Somewhere. Now after all you've had to give way.
We must calculate again, calculate without Moses.
I picked unhappy days in those girlhood rushes.
But at least we can sweep away the locusts.
  Seti.   You understand
There will be no postponement of Ramases' marriage.
We can look forward to that, and the change of fortune
Which I shall force presently. I haven't by any means
Put my policy aside.

Anath. What do you mean?
Moses by now has called the assembly of the Hebrews.
By now Egypt has heard the news. Moses
Has taken policy out of your hands.
Seti. I sent
Word after him.
Anath. Seti! What word did you send?
What have you done now against our chance
Of rest? What word did you send? Answer me, Seti!
Your promise you said this time was final. There was
No need or possibility of another word.
What have you done?
Seti. I have only been careful
To protect your future. Even before Moses
Had gone three steps from the palace there came the news
Of another defeat. Fate has taken a hammer
To chip and chip and chip at our confidence.
But while I still have Moses to come at my call
I have not lost him. And while he needs my help
He will continue to come. And when he is tired—
We'll make a bargain.
Anath. All this, then, over again.
You're mad. It isn't we who make the bargains
In this life, but chance and time. I tell you it's madness!
—Listen!
Seti. I heard nothing.
Anath. It is Teusret.

> (*She draws aside the curtain and goes on to the terrace*)

Teusret (*unseen*). Ramases!
Seti. What's the matter? She sounds afraid.
Anath. Teusret! Teusret! What has happened to you?
Teusret (*unseen*). Where is Ramases?
Where is he?

Anath.   Come here, my frightened darling.
I haven't seen Ramases. But we are here,
Your father and I.

Seti.   Is she hurt?

Anath.   She is no longer
Yesterday's Teusret. I have been watching how
She cannot altogether recognize who she now is.
Yesterday's Teusret was for yesterday's world.

Seti. She shouldn't call and cry where everyone can watch her.

(TEUSRET *comes on to the terrace.* ANATH *takes her in her arms*)

Anath. What is it? Take your head out of my heart
And tell me what it is. Each of us just now
Is an odd number with himself, but between us
We should be able to add up to something even.
Put yourself with me and see what we come to.

Teusret. Oh, Aunt!

Anath.   Can it be said?

Teusret.   Nothing can really be said,
Do you believe that? When I try for words
I disappear from myself.

Seti.   Come to me a moment, Teusret.
Now, what has frightened you? Tell me; we can't have you crying.

Teusret. My thoughts! They went—inside—the world. I don't
Seem to be able to get out. I think it's impossible
To live any more. What can I do?

Anath.   Insist on living.
More curious things happen than happiness.

Teusret. No, happiness is the most curious of all.
While I was reading, the last weeks
Came again and put their hands across
The page and closed themselves over me
Until I was inside the world. And there,
Ruling everything, is a whirlpool, trying

To escape, disguising and disguising itself,
Spitting out intricate concoctions of itself,
Shrill birds, bearded animals, heartbreaking
And perfumed flowers, delirious design
And complexity, flesh, near-flesh, seeding, seeding
To escape, with claw, voice, wing, appetite,
Beauty, fang, colour and poison, all
Nothing but a maddened beating against the walls
Of space, all consuming themselves or consuming
Others or being consumed.—And that's the sun
Rising and setting and the smooth endless
Music of the Nile. Oh the pretence
Of good when everything is hateful!
   Anath.   But you
Are not, and I hope I am not, so there
Are two things to put back into the world.
   Teusret. Aunt—
   Seti.   I have something to show you, Teusret.
We're not altogether destitute, you will see,
Of what is fine.
   Teusret.   What can you show me?
   Seti.   A vein
Of the earth. How does this seem to you?
      (*He has brought out from a casket a collar of precious stones*)
   Teusret.   O father.
Let me see! Perfect, perfect thing.
I'm too warm. Being held will melt it.
   Seti.   Drops of cornelian.
These are diamonds. Hebrew labourers dug them.
Now, Anath, you see how ill we could afford
To lose them.
   Anath.   Our grandmother wore these.
It is a pity that all the love-affairs

Between women and their jewels are broken off.

Teusret. May I wear it?

Seti.   You can try it on.

It is for Phipa when she comes.

Teusret.   The world

Is spun for Phipa! Everything for that girl!
Even these, though they seem to chatter so merrily
With the light, even these are the enemy! They go
To make Ramases welcome to her. There's beauty!

Seti. If that is how they affect you, give them back
To me.

Teusret. Take them! They were merely cast up
By the whirlpool anyway. If you can pretend
That our lives are still going on and if you can plan
Days and days of triumph because Ramases
Is going to marry a girl he has never met,
That's your own dream-story. You can't make me clap hands
And say that it's true. But you're using him for Egypt's
Purpose, and whether he's happy or unhappy
To you it's equally good. Let us alone!
You've got to let us alone!

(*She is running towards the door. Enter* RAMASES. *She cries out his name. He puts her arms gently away from him, intent on his father. She runs past him and out*)

Ramases.   Father,

Is it true you've withdrawn your latest promise to Moses?

Seti. Whatever I have done or not done isn't to be said
In a sentence.

Ramases.   They say it's true. Wherever I have gone
Dank rumour has been rising off the pavements, chilling
Into the heart of the people: "Pharaoh has refused
Moses again. What new disastrous day
Is coming?" I tell you I've been out walking

Under the burning windows of the people's eyes.
You've stood fast long enough. Let Moses take
The Hebrews.

Seti.   So you also are afraid of magic
And believe that this tall Moses can make a business
Out of curses? Do you suppose if I surrendered to him
There would be any less roaring in the wind
Or less infection in disease? Why
Aren't you beside me like another man,
Instead of so fretting me with nursery behaviour
That I could strike you? I made life in your mother
To hand me strength when I should need it. That life
Was you. I made you exactly for this time
And I find you screeching to escape it.

Ramases.   I have been
Through streets that no men should have to walk in.
You must let the Hebrews go. Father, you must!

Seti. You know nothing, you little fool, nothing! Govern
By your idiocy when I am dead.

Ramases.   What
Will you leave for me to govern, or what by then
Shall I have become, what figure of faded purple
Who clears his throat on an unimportant throne?
I am to you only the boy who comes
To the door to say goodnight on his way to bed.
It's you who invite the future but it's I
Who have to entertain it, remember that.
What is expedience for you may become
Dark experience for me. And these last weeks
I've heard the future's loping footfall, as plague
Came after plague, and I knew the steps
Were not passing but approaching. You
Were persuading them. They came each time a little

Nearer, and each time closer to me.
Keep your word to Moses. Let him take them.
  Seti. I tell you it isn't possible.
  Ramases.   Then get
Yourself another heir, and make him eat
Your black bread of policy. Marry yourself
To this girl from Syria. My plans are different.
  Seti. Your plans are different! You insolent cub, you spoiled
Insolent cub! And so your plans are different?
You've already made your plans!
  Ramases.   Wait. What
Was that noise?
  Anath.   The old familiar. A man crying out.
What difference is one man's groaning more or less?
  Ramases (*looking from the terrace*). Oh horrible! What is it that makes
    men
And makes them like this man? Abortions of nature.
It is true what they said.
  Anath.   What is true?
  Ramases. What the other officers said, what I thought they spread
About out of malice: that Shendi outstruts them all,
Drives the Hebrews harder than any Egyptian
Drives them, hits them down with a readier fist,
And smiles and thrives under the admiration
Of the overseers. Go out on the terrace if you doubt me
And see him, Shendi, the son of Miriam, a Jew
Beating a Jew.
  Seti.   So perhaps at last,
So perhaps at last you will have seen
That what you thought was child's play, black and white,
Is a problem of many sides. And you will kindly
Wait and learn. This fellow does the work
Which you yourself suggested he should do

And does it conscientiously, without sentiment.

Ramases. I suggested he should do it. Yes.
I put the whip in his hand. I raised that arm.
I struck that Jew. I did it. I did not know
How the things we do, take their own life after
They are done, how they can twist themselves
Into foul shapes. I can now see better
The deathly ground we live on. Yes, all right,
I have surrendered. Whatever happens will happen
Without me. I've finished meddling.

    Anath.   Ramases!
Of all the Jews one Jew has done this.

    Ramases.   It might be
A thousand instead of one.

    Anath.   Ramases, only
One Jew!

    Seti.   Would you even encourage the traitor
In my son, because of your fear of this Moses?

    Anath.   Yes,
I would make him rebellious, and if I could I would make
Every limb of your body rebellious;
I'd paralyse that pride which with such cunning
Packs us into a daily purgatory
Of apprehension.

    Seti.   The purgatory may save you
From damnation. But turn yourselves all against me.
I stand now living and breathing only to protect
This country from disintegration.

    Anath.   Oh
The gods, how we fumble between right and wrong,
Between our salvation and our overthrow,
Like drunk men with a key in the dark who stand
At the right door but cannot get out of the cold.

May the moment of accident bless us.

Ramases.   I shall not
Rebel again. That will be one trouble less.

Seti. Stand beside me. We're almost of equal height
And may yet come to be of equal mind;
And if that is so, one of us will find
The way of escape out of this distress
Of ours, either you or I.

(*Enter* KEF, *a Minister to the Pharaoh*)

Kef.   My lord Pharaoh.

Seti. News; come on.

Kef.   Better to hear it alone.

Seti. Bad news. Well, let's have it. Catastrophe
Is no longer my secret. Let us have it all.

Kef. My lord—

Seti.   Go on, go on,

Kef.   A report that the Libyans
Have annihilated the reinforcing fifth
Division.

Seti.   It is impossible.

Kef.   They were surrounded
And surprised. Only six men got through.

Seti.   Six men.

Ramases. Six men.

Seti.   They make me a pack-horse to carry despair.
They load me to the last inch.

(*Enter* TEUSRET)

Teusret.   Moses has come
Again. I saw him walking like a lion
Behind bars, up and down in your battered garden,
Ramases. The sentries had tried to hold him
But he broke through their spears as though he didn't see them.
He looked at me, his eyes the colour of anger;

He looked at me and gripped a mulberry-bough
And broke it, and said Go to your father, fetch me
Your father.

Seti. He can walk longer and break more boughs.
He shall wait, and find that Egypt is hard ground
Under his lion's walk. (*To* KEF) Go out to the overseers
And tell them to tighten discipline, to give
No rest to those Hebrews, not to let man, woman
Or child straighten their backs while they still stand.
I shall not see him until I choose; and, when
I choose, for his people's sake, he'll do what I need.
See this done. (*Exit* KEF)

Anath. Seti, take care; take care
What you do.

Seti. Let Moses think again what behaviour
Is best, best to save his people. (*Exit*)

Anath. And all
We can do is to wait, wait and wait in this
Uneasy entrance hall of doubtful omen,
Feeling like pale petitioners who have already
Waited beyond all bearing.

Teusret. Ramases,
What is it? Why are you so silent? Are you afraid
As well? Are you afraid? Are you, Ramases?

Ramases. Why should I be? The sweet part of the world's
All over, but that's nothing. It had to go.
My mind had lutes and harps and nodding musicians
Who drowned my days with their casual tunes. They have been
Paid off by this honest hour. And now I hear
My voice raised in deathly quiet. It's insufferable
That my voice, without the accompaniment of good fortune,
Should be so out of key, so faltering,
So cracking with puberty.—Aunt Anath,

What's the meaning of my manhood, to be found
So helpless, to be so helpless: an arbitrary thing
Of nerves and brain which this ambitious mud
We loyally call World and Planet, has spawned
Upon itself to give itself passion,
Five senses and despair. What is there to do
Which I could do and haven't yet seen?
   Anath. We're no longer alone.
                    (MOSES *stands in the doorway*)
   Teusret.   Look, Ramases.
   Moses.   Where is Seti?
   Anath. He will not see you.
   Moses.   When will he learn? When,
When, when will he learn? We have agonized
This land with anger for too many days.
   Anath.   You
And he together. No birth is worth this labour.
   Moses. For three hundred years the pangs of this coming deliverance
Have been suffered by my people, while Egypt played.
But now Egypt suffers, and she says
This is a new hell. But hell is old;
And you yourself sitting in sunlight
Embroidered on it with your needle. Hell
Is old, but until now
It fed on other women, that is all.
   Anath. And all is the innocent as well as the guilty;
All is the small farmer and the singing fisherman
And the wife who sweeps; to-morrow's boy as well
As yesterday's. All these, while Seti twists
To have his way, must go to your fire like sticks.
   Ramases (*looking from the terrace*). The gods help them now! The gods
     help those Hebrews!
   Moses. It must be one people or another, your people

Or mine. It is Seti who like a monstrous mole
Blindly throws up this mountain of pain. I
Am the conscript of an autocracy of grief.
Injuries, nursed in sullen obliterated graves,
Anguish that is lost in dust—sometime
That time-gone sea of troubled hands, my forefathers'
Martyrdom, signed me away, gave an oath for my heart
Long before I lived. And deflected purpose
Or altered ambition, or the stirred and terrible affections
Cannot discharge me. You appeal to Moses,
But Moses is now only a name and an obedience.
It is the God of the Hebrews, springing out
Of unknown ambush, a vigour moving
In a great shadow, who draws the supple bow
Of his mystery, to loose this punishing arrow
Feathered with my fate; he who in his hour
Broke the irreparable dam which kept his thought,
Released the spumy cataract birth and death
To storm across time and the world;
He who in his morning
Drew open the furious petals of the sun;
He who through his iron fingers
Lets all go, lets all waste and go,
Except, dearly retained in his palm, the soul:
He, the God of my living, the God of the Hebrews,
Has stooped beside Israel
And wept my life like a tear of passion
On the iniquity of Egypt.
    Anath. So the great general steps down to captaincy.
I wonder. Does this god use you
Or do you use this god? What is this divinity
Which with no more dexterity than a man
Rips up good things to make a different kind

Of good? For any god's sake, if you came here
To get justice, also give justice.
In this mood the lot goes headlong.

Moses.   Headlong!
And our memories too. And our hands which once
Knew how to come together, must now forever
Hide themselves in our dress. We are utterly separate.

Ramases. Look at the sky! A sea of cloud, blind-black,
Is pouring on to the beaches of the sun!

Teusret. Oh, it will swamp the sailing of the air!
The sky will be gone from us, it's taking the sky!
What shall we do?

Anath.   Hush, Teusret.

> (*The stage grows dark*)

Moses.   Seti
May see better without the light of day.
The hand of God has gone across his eyes
And closed all life upon itself. Egypt
Goes inward, by a gate which shuts more heavily than sunset,
Leaving man alone with his baffled brain.
Only Seti can let the sun free again.

Anath. It is here! The darkness!

Moses.   Tell him, tell Seti
That I wait for his answer.

CURTAIN TO ACT TWO

ACT THREE

SCENE ONE

MIRIAM's *tent at night.*   AARON.   *Enter* MIRIAM.

Aaron. Everything has been done, I think. I have daubed
The lamb's blood three times over the entry
And all that remained of the meat has been burned.—
Miriam! You; not Moses! What do you want
Here at close on midnight?

Miriam.   Must I want something
To come into my own tent?

Aaron.   Tell me; what is it?
There's no time left. Has the news got past our silence?
Do they know? That's why you've come in the night. The Egyptians
Are one ahead of us!

Miriam.   News? I've got no news.
Is there any news at midnight? I've come to sleep.

Aaron. Why not sleep, as you did, in the city with Shendi?

Miriam. Do I have to stand and be catechized in my own tent?
If you want to ferret in unlighted places
Penetrate into the mind of Moses, and let me
Sleep.

Aaron. His mind will be our history
Before the morning. Whatever is about to happen—
I cannot doubt that something is about to happen—
Will divulge him to us at last. I have become
Almost docile to his darkness. By what providence
I wonder, did you come back? There was no way
Of getting word to you, but you came, thank God.
Whatever is wrong for you, to make you walk

So far to sleep, this midnight of Moses
(I call it to myself his midnight) will clarify
Into right.
   Miriam.   Wrong things and right things!
So you still talk of those, those things that are catches
To make us lose heart. Take evil by the tail
And you find you are holding good head-downwards.
Let me go to sleep.
   Aaron.   Something that Shendi has done
Has brought you back.
   Miriam.   Shendi, Shendi to blame!
To you Shendi is always blameable.
Because at last he can have ambitions,
Because he's ripping up the bare boards
His boyhood lay on, to make himself a fire
Which will warm his manhood, we turn on him—yes,
I also, as much as you—I stormed so.
I? The right to blame him? The wrong to have borne him
To that childhood. Why shouldn't he be finished with the lot of us?
   Aaron. So he turned you out: he sent you away.
   Miriam.   I left him.
I came away from him. I couldn't watch him
Live what is now his life.
   Aaron.   I won't think of him.
   Miriam. He'll succeed without your thoughts.
   Aaron.   Look at me, Miriam.
   Miriam. You're going away.
   Aaron.   And so is all Israel.
We all have staves in our hands and our feet shod
For travelling; Moses' orders. He also gave
Other orders; they were very curious.
We have all had to eat lambs' flesh, seasoned
With bitter herbs. As I see it, Miriam,

That is his characteristic way of achieving
Unity among us, before the event,
That we should all fill this waiting time by doing
The same thing, however trivial. And then
We have splashed the blood three times over the doorways.
That is quite inexplicable. It is drying in the night air,
At this moment, while I speak. What happens, I ask myself,
When it is dry? It means our freedom. He has told me so.
To-night we're to go free. And when I look at him
I have to permit myself a wonderful hope.

  Miriam. He came back from Midian a madman.

  Aaron. His madness seems to be a kind of extended sanity.
But he tells me nothing, nothing is discussed or planned
Even with me, his lieutenant. And this closeness
Has hurt me, I won't try to deny it. And yet
He has me by the scruff of the heart and I ask
No questions. I've begun to believe that the reasonable
Is an invention of man, altogether in opposition
To the facts of creation, though I wish it hadn't
Occurred to me. I've been with Moses, watching
How in tent after tent he manipulated
Man upon man into consciousness. Though perhaps
They don't know of what they're conscious, any more than I do.
Except of the night; of the night, Miriam! I would swear
The night is dedicated to our cause.
You must have seen it: there's such a brightness,
Such a swingeing stillness, the sky has transfixed itself;
As though it hung with every vigorous star
On some action to be done before daybreak.
Is it my nerves? A sort of high apprehensive fever?
I can't discuss myself. To-morrow this glitter
And piercing peace may be something of our own.

  Miriam. Peace! Give it to me, for God's sake.

All I could see was the peace of the crouching creature
Hanging upon its pounce.

(Enter SHENDI)

Shendi.   Why must he be here?
I have something to say to you, mother.

  Miriam.   Not any more
To-night; nothing more said to-night. Go back
To your bed.

  Shendi.   Yes, you must listen!

  Aaron.   Listen to your tongue
Or your brotherly whip?

  Miriam.   He knows already what we feel.
Now let him alone.

  Shendi.   Let him think what he likes. I have come
To you, not to him. We've taken so long to get
What at last we have: why must you spoil it? I know;
It was the spate of our tempers, gone again now.
If you go away from me, more than half the triumph
Is lost. You haven't been my mother for nothing.
I mean to see you happy.

  Miriam.   I shall stay alone.

  Shendi. Oh, it's fantastic. What did you expect
My work to be? And how can we be scrupulous
In a life which, from birth onwards, is so determined
To wring us dry of any serenity at all?

  Miriam. You must do as you must.

  Aaron.   But in the morning
He may wish he had chosen otherwise.

  Shendi.   What do you mean?
Let me hear what you mean by that. Have you
And your brother done some dirtiness against me
To put me wrong with the Pharaoh? I know you'd founder me
If you had the chance—

(*Enter* MOSES)

Moses.   Get ready. Miriam. And you,
Shendi. Get together all that you value.
You won't come to this tent again.

Miriam.   Get ready?
All that I value? What would that be, I wonder?
Tell your delirium to be precise.

Aaron. This midnight is his. For pity's sake believe it,
Miriam. Then all our wills resolved into
One Will—

Shendi.   His, of course! The stupendous mischief
Of the man! I beg your pardon if he no longer
Rates himself as a man after living through
The pestilences as though he owned them.
You can blame him, not me, for the punishment
I give the labourers. He makes them undisciplined
With his raving of freedom which they'll never get.
It's he, not I, who knits the darker and darker
Frowns for Pharaoh—it's he who's the one for you
To abominate, if anybody.

Moses.   Be ready for journey.
The time is prepared for us. What we were is sinking
Under the disposition of what will be.
Let it so dispose; let us not fondle our wrongs
Because they're familiar. Now, as the night turns,
A different life, pitched above our experience
Or imagining, is moving about its business.
To-night—Aaron, Miriam, Shendi—our slavery
Will be gone.

Aaron.   Do you hear what he says?

Miriam.   What is he hiding?
There's something he knows.

Aaron.   Something known by the night;

That was how it felt to me.

Shendi.   Come out of this,
Mother. They need more room to foam and splutter in.
If you come back with me you know you can be sure
Of a rational world of pleasant men and women.
Isn't that so? You don't want to stay here.

Miriam. I want to know why he's standing there, so certain
That something will happen to-night. What does he know?

Shendi. The shape of his own mouth.

Aaron.   Confidence
In what he knows, but not in us, alas;
Not in me. The advance begins, and I am in command
Of my perfect ignorance. Moses, tell me, is that
How it is to be?

Miriam.   What is it you know?

Moses.   The sound
Of God. It comes; after all, it comes. It made
The crucial interchange of earth with everlasting;
Found and parted the stone lips of this
Egyptian twilight in the speech of souls,
Moulding the air of all the world, and desiring
Into that shell of shadow, a man's mind—
Into my own. Only now, only
Now, Aaron, as it moves away,
Can I try to form it to you. Miriam,
This is what I know, and how I know what comes
To-night.

Miriam. Am I to believe it? Isn't this no more
Than I thought it would be: the thumping of the frenzy in him?

Aaron. What was told? What was said?

Shendi.   Oh, leave them
To excite each other. I'm going if you're not. Perhaps
By to-morrow you'll see reason. I'll come back then.

Moses. Stay where you are. Can you comprehend
That we're sometimes hoisted by the unbelievable
On to the shoulders of truth? Our custom is
To live backward of reality. When it turns its face
How can it be recognized? But a refusal
Of recognition is like a cancellation
Of our existence. Do you deny voice
To that power, the whirler of suns and moons, when even
Dust can speak, as it does in Moses now?
It comes. And by the welding of what loved me
And what harmed me, I have amazingly been brought
To that stature which has heard. To-night, at midnight,
God will unfasten the hawk of death from his
Grave wrist, to let it rake our world,
Descend and obliterate the firstborn of Egypt,
All the firstborn, cattle, flocks, and men:
Mortality lunging in the midnight fields
And briding in the beds: a sombre visit
Such as no nation has known before. Upon
All Egypt! Only we who have the darkness
Here in our blood, under the symbol of blood
Over our doors, only we of Israel
Standing ready for the morning will be unvisited.

Aaron. So this is what you know.

Shendi. What he wants, what he fondly
Imagines. Is he so dull he can't see the risk
Of heaving this up in front of me? An officer
Of Egypt. He may have forgotten it.

Aaron. I should say this is no night to be an Egyptian.

Miriam. There will never be this midnight! It will still
Stop short of us!

Shendi. Why did I follow you here
To get drawn into this? That fox has his tail on fire

And someone should know about it. For the last time,
Are you coming?

Miriam.   Don't go back—not just
Within a pace of this midnight; Shendi, not now
When I've lost the knack of knowing sense from nonsense.
The city, for my peace of mind, can find its way
Over midnight without you.

Shendi.   I can see
What's been thought out between you. Were you the decoy
To fetch me here? And now that you have me away
You think you'll keep me: here, dropped back in the pit.
What a chance of it! Must I tell you that I'm an Egyptian?
An Egyptian! I'm an Egyptian! Now what becomes
Of your craftiness and your birdlime?

Miriam.   No! No!
The midnight is in us before it comes; it comes to us
Out of ourselves! I didn't know that you would follow me.
You're scoring your own heart for nothing, for nothing,
Shendi. I only ask you to wait until midnight
Is safely past us.

Aaron.   Soon enough now; before
We know where we are.

Shendi.   Do you think you can make a fool of me?
Do I look so very credulous? Don't I know
How he's waited for me to slip up, because he
Slipped up?

Moses.   Break and finish that! With every ram
Of your intelligence, break that jealous, bitter
And scheming puppet you have dubbed with my name.
Are you going to let the non-existing
Dog and destroy your existence? That Moses in your head
Is a lie.

Shendi. What does it matter whether he is

Or he isn't? You want to bring Egypt down,
To fell her with the weight of her own achievement.
What else but Egypt is able to make birth
A proposition? You aim to destroy excellence
For what you call a justice. Justice
Is the greatness that comes to the great!

Moses.   It's the crossing of mind
With mind. How can I make you see me, clear
Of what you want to believe?

Shendi.   I see you well enough.
You've taken ten years looking for the logic of your murder
And now you think you've found it.

Aaron.   Midnight, midnight!
Have you both forgotten it? No doubt the timing of God
Will be extremely exact. But in fact we realize
Nothing. If it comes, how completely
Shall we realize it then? And does nothing, no presentiment,
Creep on the heart of Pharaoh at this moment?
I wonder, does nothing make him fetch his firstborn
Beside him—

Moses.   Aaron!

Miriam.   Shendi, let me keep you here
For one hour only, to protect me from panic.

Moses.   Aaron!
Do you see the ambush I have blundered into?
I heard God, as though hearing were understanding.
But he kept his hands hidden from me. He spoke,
But while he spoke he pointed. Aaron, he pointed
At Ramases, and I couldn't see!

Aaron.   The boy
Pays for the father, as though we bred in order
To redeem ourselves.

Moses.   Why had I not thought of him?

I had such tremendous heart. It seemed at last
As though we had reached the breaking of the seals,
When we no longer should be set down blindfold
To build upon light. I saw the passion of bewilderment
Drawing off from the earth. But can we go forward
Only by the ravage of what we value? Surely
I who have been the go-between for God
Can say that this is not part of my intention
And be heard?

   Aaron.   What, at this point? Is this how you fought
Your other wars? There were boys then who put
Eager toes into fatal stirrups, who were young
And out of life altogether in the same
Almighty and unthinkable moment. You learnt
Then to grieve and advance, uninterrupted.
And so it has to be now.

   Moses.   If it were the same!
But I am stealing Ramases without warning
And handing him to oblivion. Look what it is.
God is putting me back with the assassins.
Is that how he sees me? Does one deed
Become our immortal shape? And Egypt! Egypt!
He was meant for Egypt. If I have any freedom
More than the freedom of my thoughts, I must make
Providence mutual with my world of sense,
Or else I shall become wandering in my soul.
Ramases must be dragged clear of this runaway
Misconceiving miracle of God.
It isn't he that I shall be forced to spend
To get the fulfilment of what I do! Aaron,
You are here in my place until I come again.
Keep Shendi with you.

   Aaron.   Where are you going?

Moses.   To the palace.

Aaron. What will you do? Am I to be left midstream
Of a miracle, not even knowing what it portends?

Moses. Do nothing but watch the night become day. All happens.
I have to know what I am. Keep Shendi with you.   (*He goes*)

Aaron. He is in a space somewhere between
The human and inhuman. That's a terrible
Neighbourhood.

Shendi.   Did you see how he looked? He believes
What he said. He looked a ghost haunting his face.
He believes it all—like a child.

Miriam.   Shut us in. He has gone.
Can't we forget the man?

Shendi.   I won't stay here!
The place is putrid with childishness. I won't stay!
Thank goodness I can go where things are healthier,
Where I can wake a few men and get myself back
To normal.

Miriam.   You know I was born to be uneasy;
I kindle dragons. Shendi, come away
From that questionable air outside.

Aaron.   It's midnight.
Wasn't that the winding of the city's horn,
The sound of twelve? I think so. I have to delay you,
Shendi.

Shendi (*at the tent-opening*). Nobody will delay me.

Miriam.   Stay in the tent!

Aaron. The hour may go past and leave us knowing
It was unremarkable. But wait till the light,
Wait, Shendi, keep yourself unseen
By that inquisition of stars out there.
Wait for Moses to return.

Shendi.   Who?

Miriam. What is it? What have you seen?

Shendi.   I've lost the city,
I can't reach it! You trapped me!

Miriam.   What do you see?

Shendi. The sand is rising and living! Do not let it
Happen. It can't, it can't rise without a wind.
Is an invisible nation going through to the north?
Or what is it the sand can feel? I can't go back,
God, God, I can't go!

Miriam.   Come inside,
Shendi, come into the tent.

Aaron.   Happening,
You see, happening. Why try to go back?

Shendi. Some of the men will still be awake. We could light
The lights in the barrack-room. If only some of them
Would come out to look for me! But who'd come now?
Do you see how the sand is wavering upright, disturbed—
Disturbed in God's name by what? It's by the passing
Of a trance of eagles! Can you hear it, the noise,
The rending apart and shuddering-to of wings?
Where can I get away from this? Nowhere
Except into the ground.

Miriam.   Shendi, here, in the tent.
In the tent: it will pass the tent.

Aaron (*dragging him in*).   Are you trying to die?'

Shendi. Let me go, death; death, let me go!

Aaron.   It is I
Not death.

Shendi.   It isn't only you.
The wings were right over me and I was wrenched by a hand
That came spinning out of them. I'll not be sent into a grave.
I'll be what I was. I am Shendi, a Jew.
How can my blood alter and make me Egyptian?

I only wanted to be free! (*He tears off the insignia of Egypt*)
Look: Egypt comes away—it's no part of me,
It's easily off. This body is all I am—
It is Shendi, the Jew, Shendi, Shendi, a Jew,
A Jew! Isn't it so? Then why am I dying?
  Miriam. You are not, Shendi; it's gone past us. There's nothing more.
  Aaron. Look, you're with us.
  Shendi.   Only free to die?
This wasn't a world. It was death from the beginning.
Here's my name, without a man to it. My name!
Let me go. It's a chance! I'll make them see me. Wings,
                        (*He breaks away into the dark*)
Shadows, eagles! I am Shendi, Shendi, the Jew!
I am Shendi the Jew! Shendi the Jew!
  Miriam.   Shendi!
He has gone behind the sand. Son! (*She runs into the dark*)
  Aaron.   The night
Of deliverance. To-night we all go free.
And Miriam too. He said she would go free.
(*The voice of* MIRIAM *is heard crying out her last desperate "Shendi!"*)

CURTAIN

SCENE TWO

The Palace.   ANATH.   TEUSRET.

  Teusret. Are you casting about in the night for sleep?
Try well beyond the terrace. Here there isn't
Even the swimming of minnow drowsiness.
I have to be stark awake, tired or not.
  Anath. One restless spirit in the house is enough.
What is the matter?
  Teusret.   If you could tell me that

Perhaps I might sleep. Listen to those men
Singing in the streets, and two women, or one?
"I'm waiting where you left me."—Are all the souls
In the city looking for sleep? Can there be nights
When sleep doesn't exist at all? Please hold me.
It is only that I've lost my way in myself.

   Anath. There come those times—maybe this is one of them—
When, as though we were trespassing on the credible,
We're driven off from the blind poise of custom
And see the unnerving, profound chasm
Between ourselves and creation: we, human,
(That singular expense of nature) lapped
And perpetuated by a universe
Of inhumanity. So, to befriend ourselves,
We give limbs to our thoughts of the gods. I find
It is easier believing the gods exist
Than believing that men do. A living body is stranger
Than a spirit. How shall we comfort ourselves? We can only
Sound our curious notes, without expecting
Any mating answer from any world,
Content to be a snatch of ambiguity,
Disturbing eternity with a kind of music.

   Teusret. If only my life would speak lower, or more
Deliberately and yet still be bright, more like
That routine of fire up there, the night's
Commonplace of stars.

   Anath.   How they have taken
Possession of the sky to-night.

   Teusret.   Occasion,
Dear Aunt. Phipa is coming, the magnitude
Out of Syria.

   Anath.   To-morrow.

   Teusret.   No; now they say to-night.

Very soon, for Ramases. Messengers were here
Half an hour ago, sweating in the cool yard.
She's already at Hahiroth, with her romantic nature
Plying the spurs and waking all the poor villages
With the interminable jingle-jangle of what father calls
Her considerable means. We shall see her
To-night.

   Anath. How do we welcome her? Nothing has been said
To me.

   Teusret. Who says anything in this palace now
Except good morning or good night? Father
Waits for each moment to come and touch him, and then
It has gone before he can use it.

   Anath.   Is it Phipa's
Coming that made sleep impossible?

   Teusret. Will you believe me? I'm praying her here. I fetch her
To Ramases, with prayers like the grip of a moon
On the long tide of her caravan. Don't you see?
She will bring solid and gay Syria
Among the fiends that sway the walls here. Aunt,
She'll bedizen nightmare until it sinks, will she not?

   Anath. I haven't weighed the power of the blandishment
Of diamonds.

(Enter SETI)

   Teusret.   Who is that?

   Seti.   I. Is there something
To be seen?

   Anath.   We're watching the dark for bridles.

   Teusret.   And the dark
Watches us. I know you dislike me to be afraid of it.
Are we all to meet her in the jumping shadows,
Aunts, owls, flame, sisters and all?
Or will she go quietly to bed and wait for to-morrow?

Seti. To-night. She must dismount into a light
Of welcome. Where's your brother? Turn this way;
Are you handsome? Well, the years of my life
Conveyed in a woman, perhaps safely. Remember to love me
For everything you become, particularly
For the worship of the male sunrise which will stand
Over your maturity.

  Teusret.   What is it, father?
What is it?

  Seti.   How many thousand thousand years
Are being nursed in your body, my young daughter?
And under a secure lock, away from the eyes.

  Teusret. What eyes?

  Seti.   The envy; confusion. Do you know
Where to look for Ramases?

  Teusret.   He was trying to sleep.
What is it that is wrong?

  Seti.   The world's constitution.
Otherwise everything is much as we would wish it.
I'll tell you what is wrong. The world is a wonder
Married to some deformity; but we'll fetch them
Apart. Where is Ramases?

  Teusret.   In bed.

  Seti. He can go to bed to-morrow.

  Anath.   Precious heart,
That was a wild cry that ripped the darkness
From somewhere down in the city. Did you hear it?

  Seti. He will have dreams in a host after to-night;
I'm giving them to him with both my hands. Where is he?
Fetch him.

  Ramases (*in the doorway*). I am here, sir.

  Seti.   You're the Pharaoh.

  Anath. Seti!

Seti.   Egypt is a child again.
Have I been as young as this? You have slept
Into a throne and an empire, while time has begun
To heap age over me with a bony spade
To make me like the rest, Ramases, like
The poor rest.
　　Ramases.   Has Syria come?
　　Anath.   Tell the boy
What you mean: and me. What are you pulling down now?
　　Seti. Myself. It seems that I have grown too tall
And keep out the sun. I overbranch the light.
I am giving you the throne, Ramases.
It gives itself. The wind has hurled it under you,
A biting wind, the hatred that has turned me
Into storm, decay and grub in my own garden.
You may have luckier hands. You have at least
Hands less calloused with enemies. You will be able
To hold the sceptre perhaps without such pain.
　　Anath. Abdication!
　　Ramases.   Is that what you mean? The throne.
Earth's ruin is to become my region.
　　Seti. What? Come out of your sleep. Are you going to mope
Good gold away as though it were sand in glass?
We're in time. Aren't you myself again? Listen to me:
This is how we distract them: under my seal
Affixed in the morning, Moses shall be given the permission
He has raged for: and then, with the sun somewhat higher,
Under my final seal you shall take Egypt.
I drown myself in my own wave: I am not,
But I am always. And when they come, the factions,
The whorers and devourers, roaring over
The rocks of the dynasty, they'll only find
Perpetual Egypt.

Anath.   Like a haven of sand.
But that's for me, not for these two children.
For them I'll believe in hope, or the hope of hope.
  Seti. Hope? What has Egypt to do with hope,
That dwindled and dingy prayer? You long ago
Drove yourself out of your rights, and made yourself
Servile in some thankless kingdom of your head.
Is my abjuration of the bright
Wrists of the world, on which the centuries
Are bracelets, expected to fetch us only hope?
I am delivering Egypt up to my son.
Shouldn't that buy off apprehension for ever?
Do none of you understand what I'm sacrificing?
  Ramases. Yes: whatever was prefigured in time
To be my life. I'm to inherit the kingdom
Of desperate measures, to be not a self
But a glove disguising your hand. Is there nowhere
Where I can come upon my own shape
Between these overbearing ends of Egypt?
Where am I to look for life?
  Seti.   But what
Am I shaking over you if not a wealth
Of life? Do you comprehend, this land of cities
Lying dazed with time's faithfulness
Is yours? And the heart of beauty out of Syria.
Teusret, watch; is there anything to be seen?
Any sound yet?—Stupidity, what would you have?
Love is the dominant of life, to which all our changes
Of key are subdued in the end. You will be able
To wander the winding and coitous passages
Of the heart, and be more than you could have prophesied
For yourself.
  Teusret. The singing in the street has stopped;

But now, something else—

Seti.   Well, what? Is it the girl?

Anath. Listen!

Teusret.   A tortured gale, a gale of crying
Moving up through the streets! Oh no! no!

Seti. Crying of what?

Anath.   Has the earth found voice
At last to bring compassion to the nail-thrusts
Of those glaring stars?

Teusret.   It's the noise of breaking lives!
Isn't it so?

Anath.   As though the roots of faith
Were being dragged out of the live flesh of the land.

Teusret. We're together, Ramases, some way, or is no one
Ever with another? Your hand feels wise. And now
Mine is part of it. So much for fear!
We're locked against whatever is there in the city.

Ramases. Teusret, what is there may be ourselves
Coming to find us; we have to listen to it.

Seti. What is it now? Has evil so many rat-holes
We can't stop them up? In the name of the soul,
How can we caulk a world which is such a sieve
To darkness?

Ramases.   What is it, Darkness?

Anath.   Oh, make the city
Silent! Did you see that? The shape of a man
Leaping for the terrace?

Seti.   Get back into the room!
Back! Here is treachery's shadow in the shadow.

Ramases. Let it come to me, then. If I'm to have Egypt
I'll have its treachery as well. Keep
Away from the window. Who goes there? Stand.
Who goes there? Who is it?

(MOSES *comes breathlessly on to the terrace*)

Moses.   Shut all your doors!
Nothing will wait for us, we are at war
With this moment, draw yourselves like swords. It is
For Ramases. Put your lives round him.

Anath. My life? Who has my life? Find it.

Ramases.   For me?

Seti. Have you come out of the city? What is there?
Show your hand, even with the ace of terror.
What is on its way to us?

Moses.   Death, death, deliberately
Aimed, falling on all your firstborn sons,
All Egypt's firstborn, Seti, cattle and men;
Death particular and infallible, mounting
With an increasing terrible wake of cries
To your window, to come to Ramases. I know—
It was I that loosed it. Can I deflect it now?
Can we so rope our lives together that we
Can be a miracle against death?

Seti.   Go back
Into your night! I don't believe in you.
You are a figment of the insupportable,
Face of a lie. Go back out of belief.

Anath. He can't, can't, can't! He is caught with us,
Like us, in the falling tower of time. He is true;
And I give him my desperation to do what he may with.
Will that save Ramases?

Teusret.   But who has condemned him?
What has he done? Has he made too much love
In the world? What guilt do you want us to clear him of?
Oh we can, easily, easily!

Ramases.   My own death
Is near to me. I hear what you all say

But all I can feel is that the night will be heavy,
Awkward with goodbyes. Death, it appears,
Tells nothing upon its beaches, has no breeze
Explaining to the land, nor even a kiss
Of warning salt, or frail disposal of spray
To hint at such huge water. Can it rise
So darkly over the sand without a sound?
Perhaps this is its hand that seems to be passing
Through my hair, feeling for the skull.
An utter end of all the neighbourhood
Of light and yet there is nothing I understand.
Is it my action? Or an action done to me?
And do I live by this, because of this,
For this only?
  Teusret.   Ramases, you're believing
It will come! Then if it does, life is wicked,
Life will deserve death.
  Seti.   But I have changed
The channel that evil was running in. The boy
Is the Pharaoh. What has set humanity tolling
Now? It has no reason to.
  Moses.   The Pharaoh?
  Ramases. Is it too late, no use after all?
  Moses.   We'll hold you
With our lives, if our lives will hold, and if before midnight
We can only pass to each other safely. In life's
Name, what are we? Five worlds of separation?
Or can we be five fingers to close into
A hand, to strike this night clean away from us?
There must be no thin place left for death
To arrow through to him.
  Anath.   How can we be in time?
Are we all as lost within ourselves

As this?

Teusret. Father, the crying-out! Quickly, quickly,
It is so near!

Seti.   I will do anything.
But all direction is gone.

Ramases.   Perhaps it is
My own deed after all. Then no one can change it.

Moses. All was right, except this, all, the reason,
The purpose, the justice, except this culmination.
God, now good has turned on itself and become
Its own enemy. Have we to say that truth is only
Punishment? What *must* we say to be free
Of the bewildering mesh of God?

Anath.   What do you want from us?

Moses. Power of life, to beat death out of this house.

Anath. Say what it is! Say what is my life?
It went to be your shadow. For fifteen years
It has been nothing but a level of darkness
Cast on the world by you. I was the cheat
Of my own heart, who made myself your mother
And then loved you and desired you, until you became
The world's bruise and ease, the blessing and torment,
The water that kept me alive to thirst.
Is this the power you can use against death?

Moses. This isn't what we must say—not now!

Anath.   What else?
Ramases must live! At last, at last
You need something of me. Ramases must live.
Can the power of my unsleeping madness—
That burning beauty and insidious worm
Of hunger—can my love for you get him
From death? If it will, let it enrich itself
On that; but what power has it that can never know

If you could have loved me? Merely to have known
How little or much I strangled, how near I was
To peace? But fear shapes and changes us
And becomes our only courage, and I was afraid
For you to know you were not my son, for then
I should have lost even that right in you.
And so the world has been one thing and I another,
And the life in me has kept me out of life.

Moses. Anath—

Anath.   I loved you until I longed to hear
That you were dead.

Moses.   What can we make
Of the old circling peewit of our past
That whimpers for the breast of the dry moon
And keeps a querulous twilight, year and year?
More life! The dark is already pacing us.
Must we be agents of this deadly visit
Of God? Give me greater life, for the boy's sake!

Ramases. But how should I wear life now? It has become
Something too large to put on. If I'm to live
Shall I know how?

Seti.   Yes, ask, son of myself;
Ask that! There's life in questions. But pray
With your soul that you receive no answers.
My branch, my Ramases, on to your knees.
Truth will be the finish, the disaster.
Our power and progress is our being free
Of truth. Do you think I haven't known
That it's the immortal lying of our spirits
Gives the unpromising earth the look of excellence?
Am I to deride myself away
Into what I am, futility?
Sufficient illusion is sufficient life.

No one will persuade me
That I must break my heart with truth.

Ramases. And in your prime of illusion I was begotten.
It's fair enough I should be dispelled. Gods,
I'm tired of thinking. If it were here and quick
I should stop trembling.

Moses.   Has none of us the life
To keep him living? Pain of man, iron
Of nature without record, sacrifice, faith,
Storm-riding souls and rearing of spirit,
Are we the way through, letting in destruction?
Affirm and succeed into my strength to lock me
Equally with this wrestler rising out of midnight.

Teusret. Look, look—the torches in the gateway.
She is here! We shall be alive again.
Phipa has come to us, and the shawms have begun
To wind their welcome in the towers. Come on,
Ramases, come to meet her.

Seti.   Anath, all of you,
We meet her as though Egypt were in high health.
No anxiety in your faces as of ambassadors
Of a haunted country. Is it the main body
Or only the advance riders?

Teusret.   Ramases,
Are we going? The dark's not dangerous now.

Ramases. But still dark. And we have to enact a daylight
For this unsuspecting beauty. How easy is that?
Well, for the stairs, then. We'll meet her.

Anath.   No,
Don't go, don't look! Moses, it is now
That you must break in on to your powers.
Now, now! What strength have you? I saw—

Moses. I am nothing!

Anath.   There were men, opening the gates,
Who fell and still are lying there, and an owl
In mid-air wrenched itself upward screaming and smashed
Down on to the yard—there's another! Oh,
The bat that flew by me now, has dropped from sight!—
Are these the flowers we throw to a bride? Of the birds
The shouts and neighing wakened, many are falling
Dead; one has struck a torch from a man's
Hand. It is here!

Moses.   The shadows are too many.
Where is my hand to go to? Ramases,
There's no more of me than this. This is all.
I followed a light into a blindness.

Teusret. Come away, Ramases, Ramases
Come now, now. You must meet her and love her.
Isn't it in love that life is strongest?
I want you to love her. Already we're late.

Ramases. Why is she sighing, Teusret? Such great sighs.
They have taken all the air. Now there will be
Nowhere to breathe. Come with me. (*He crumples and falls*)

Teusret.   Ramases!
I don't know the way!

Ramases.   I am finding it for you.

Moses. Ramases, can you forget life
So quickly? This is my hand, a living hand;
Do you remember? Still be as this hand is,
Like this and this.

Ramases.   Stoop, Teusret. You see?
You cannot lose me. Here I am. (*He dies*)

Teusret. Oh, help me to take him to her, make him see her
Ramases, we're to go to the stairs. Listen,
That shouting is in Syrian. How can he hear,
With his head so? I had a secret to bring you

When you marry. Ramases! I'll meet her alone, then.
Coming in she'll reach you—must, must.
She came so far. (*She runs to the courtyard*)

  Moses.   This is how it is
To make time your friend. The earth has come and gone.
For him the earth has gone. But for us it still
Hangs in the air, like a smell of burning
Which must be searched for, so slight, but we cannot rest
Until, like this, we have put it out.

  Seti. What's that movement? The light touching his ring.
Is that all the life you have for me now?
Light, there are his eyes. Go to them again.
Why will you waste on a stone? A stone. Stone.

  Anath. Is death the last illusion, Ramases,
Pharaoh of sleep? O darling hope,
You have become my promise. Keep it, unbroken.
You have the one possession of the world.

  Moses. An end? Why should he die again in us?
Live in us, Ramases, in what years we can have for you.

  Seti (turning on MOSES). You have done what you returned for. You
came in the morning.
Leave us with what remains of the night.
No man in Egypt will prevent you. The day
You found us in is over.

  Anath. You have the freedom of the darkness, Moses.
Why do you wait? Haven't you recognized
The triumph of your purpose? Your twelve hundred
Thousand souls, out there in the dungeon of the night,
Are waiting to hear the long bolts grate back.
Ramases has died, and the air stands
Ready in the wilderness to take you in.
Ramases has died. To-morrow the lizards
Will be sparkling on the rocks. Why aren't you dancing

With such liberty for such starving souls?

Moses. I do not know why the necessity of God
Should feed on grief; but it seems so. And to know it
Is not to grieve less, but to see grief grow big
With what has died, and in some spirit differently
Bear it back to life. The blame could impale me
For ever; I could be so sick of heart
That who asked for my life should have it; I could believe
Creation to be no more than a weight of stone
Quarried for the chisel of doom; or I could see
Man's life go forward only by guilt and guilt.
Then we should always watch Ramases dying,
Whereas he had such life his death can only
Take him for a moment, to undo his mortality,
And he is here pursuing the ends of the world.
There is a wilderness between my blood and peace.
But what does eternity bear witness to
If not at last to hope? Eternal failure
Would make creation void before the void
Had seen creation. Anath—Egypt—
Why should it have been I that had to be
Disaster to you? Now, always unknown
To each other, we must force the arduous, damnable
Pass of time. Farewell.

Anath. You were wrong, wrong!
You will have nothing now except the wilderness.
It's all your future and your old age. Oh, take
Your shadow off me. I shall remember only
What I have loved and make to-morrow of that.

Moses. Somehow the pulse of living mustn't falter.
Is that enough to carry into the wilderness?
We must each find our separate meaning
In the persuasion of our days

Before we meet in the meaning of the world.
Until that time.

                 (*He goes.*   *Re-enter* TEUSRET)

  Teusret.   I have seen her. How can she be
Too late? Is beauty not a wand? Then
We shall live again. Oh Ramases,
I'm Teusret. Are you so taken with the dark
That what has dazzled me won't open your eyes?
I have whispered into your sleep at other times
And you've heard me.—Ramases,
She has come so gifted for you, possessing
A fable of rubies, and pearls like seeds of the moon,
With metal and strange horns, ebon and ivory,
Spilling chalcedonyx and male sapphires.
Doesn't their brightness come to you? Do they glimmer
Nowhere into the cupboards of your sleep?

  Seti. She need bring nothing, except the hour that has gone.

CURTAIN

END OF THE PLAY

CPSIA information can be obtained at www.ICGtesting.com
Printed in the USA
LVOW11s1932270214

375436LV00001B/27/P